Contents

Introduction

This book sets out to provide advice, guidance and practical ideas to ensure that children with special educational needs and disabilities are helped to achieve their full potential within a fully inclusive environment. The majority of children with an identified special educational need are educated in mainstream schools. In January 2010, 90% of the 1.7 million pupils identified with special educational needs were in maintained, mainstream schools. Since 2003, the proportion of pupils with a statement of special educational needs has slightly decreased from 3.0% to 2.7%, whilst the proportion identified as needing less intensive additional support at School Action or School Action Plus has increased from 14.0% in 2003 to 18.2% in 2010. *(Department for Education 2010. DfE: Special educational needs in England).*

> **The Special Educational Needs Code of Practice defines special needs as:**
> 'Children have special educational needs if they have a learning difficulty which calls for special educational provision to be made for them.
>
> Children have a learning difficulty if they:
>
> (a) Have a significantly greater difficulty in learning than the majority of children of the same age; or
>
> (b) Have a disability which prevents or hinders them from making use of educational facilities of a kind generally provided for children of the same age in schools within the area of the local education authority
>
> (c) Are under compulsory school age and fall within the definition at (a) or (b) above or would so do if special educational provision was not made for them.
>
> *(Department for Education 2001. Special Educational Needs Code of Practice. Nottinghamshire: HMSO, page 12.)*

Through the process of observation and assessment, teachers may identify particular children who are not making expected progress and have specific or general learning difficulties. When this is the case, teachers need to inform the school's Special Educational Needs Coordinator (SENCO) of their concerns about a particular child. The role of the SENCO is to implement the SEN Code of Practice model of action and intervention. The SENCO can then provide teachers with advice and guidance on how to provide differentiated learning opportunities, on appropriate teaching materials, and on how to organise the classroom so that the child can learn effectively.

The SEN Code of Practice states that:

'Most children admitted to an infant or primary school will already have attended an early education setting. Some will not. Children with special educational needs who have attended a nursery class, playgroup or other early education setting should have had their needs identified already. Others may not. Schools should therefore be aware that any child admitted to the reception class might have unidentified special educational needs. The same applies to children who transfer from one school to another during the primary phase.'

(Department for Education 2001. Special Educational Needs Code of Practice. Nottinghamshire: HMSO, page 44, para 5.1)

This book provides practical advice and guidance that will be of value to both the SENCO and the classroom teacher. Teachers use the curriculum to plan their teaching, organising their learning environments and daily routines to ensure that they provide the best climate for learning. The majority of children thrive within these classrooms. Children generally fit with relatively little adjustment into this carefully planned provision – what might be referred to as the 'round pegs fitting into round holes'. The majority of children fit comfortably into this 'round hole'. However, when the child's needs are different from the majority, or their needs have a different 'shape', this presents us with challenges. For successful inclusion it is vital that we strive to change the shape or nature of the provision (the 'round hole') rather than the 'shape' of the child (the 'peg'). In other words, we must adapt the curriculum, the learning environment, resources, daily routines and expectations to ensure that no matter what 'shape' the 'pegs' (children) are, they all fit and thrive within the inclusive classroom.

Consider the following scenario concerning Tom, aged six. He never sits still during carpet time. He wriggles and generally disturbs other children, and he refuses to sit with his legs crossed like the rest of the children in his class. Despite the teacher constantly reinforcing her expectations of 'good sitting', 'good listening' and 'good looking', he appears to ignore her prompts. The teacher eventually becomes frustrated by his behaviour. Because of his apparent non-compliance, he is an irritation to her and to the rest of the class. As a consequence of his non-compliance, Tom is often asked to stay in and loses part of his playtime. This is an example of where the 'square peg' (Tom) is expected to fit into the 'round hole' (the provision). Tom is being asked to do what all the children in the class can easily do – that is, to sit cross-legged on the carpet and concentrate for ten minutes. The scenario above demonstrates unwillingness by the teacher to change or differentiate her expectations for that child (the shape of 'the hole'). The teacher needs to consider why Tom is not complying – he may, for example, have undiagnosed dyspraxia. If this is the case, he will be unable to keep his body still or to be able to coordinate his limbs into a 'crossed-leg' position. If he does, indeed, have dyspraxia, all of his effort and concentration will be needed to try and control his movements in order to please the teacher. This may be the reason why he is unable to sit still and pay attention to the lesson.

Tom presents with 'difference' in his behaviour. If the teacher were to look at the behaviour of the child to find the reason for it, rather than concentrating on the behaviour itself, then she might try some of the following actions or strategies:

- Allow Tom to lean against a wall with enough space to stretch his legs out.

- Provide Tom with a special mat or a wobble cushion to sit on and to firmly establish bodily contact with the floor.

- Ignore the fidgeting where possible.

- Explain to the other children Tom's need for space and his need for encouragement to pay attention.

- Provide Tom with a 'fiddle object' e.g. a pipe cleaner or a piece of play dough.

Through the introduction of the above strategies, the teacher is changing the 'shape' or nature of the provision and adjusting her expectations of the 'peg' (Tom).

The scenario on the previous page gives an example of how one teacher might recognise and respond to a child with dyspraxia. Within any classroom, there might be children with identified or unidentified special needs. For the teacher who has no or limited experience of working with children with special needs, the challenge of providing an environment and curriculum appropriate for the needs of all children might seem an impossible task. To support teachers, especially those working in the early years, Chapter 1 of the book gives a list of indicators that can be used as an initial frame of reference for the early identification and intervention process. Once a special educational need is identified, Chapters 2–8 will provide the teacher with strategies, ideas and resources to help them to improve the teaching environment (the shape of the 'hole') and expectations within the curriculum. The ultimate goal is to include all children within the learning provision so that each child has the opportunity to be fully included in the learning process as a valued member of the class.

What is inclusion?

All children are entitled to full access to a broad and balanced curriculum within a setting that is appropriate to their needs. The detailed guidance in the SEN Code of Practice is informed by the following principle: 'a stronger right for children with SEN to be educated at a mainstream school' (*Department for Education 2001. Special Educational Needs Code of Practice. Nottinghamshire: HMSO,* page 7, para 1.5). This suggests that where possible, all children should be educated within mainstream provision. Children with a higher level of need will require a more targeted approach, which can be provided by specialist provision.

The National Curriculum Statutory Inclusion Statement (Department for Education 2008) emphasises the importance of providing effective learning opportunities for all pupils and offers three key principles for inclusion:

1. Setting suitable learning challenges.

2. Responding to pupils' diverse needs.

3. Overcoming potential barriers to learning and assessment for individuals and groups of pupils.

Inclusion **is not** about:

● Seeing the child (the 'square peg') as a problem.

● The child simply being part of a class where the provision and practice do not reflect the individual needs of the child.

● Using the same systems and approaches for every child.

● The child having frequent one-to-one sessions outside the classroom.

● Providing a support assistant to shadow the child constantly.

● Focusing solely on what the child can't do.

Inclusion **is** about:

● Believing that all children are individuals and have equal rights.

● Believing that every child has the right to have their needs met within a mainstream setting.

● Seeing difficulties as 'challenges' to be overcome.

● Making the learning environment fully accessible.

● Differentiating activities to meet the needs of each child.

● Providing the opportunity for each child to access all aspects of school life.

● Encouraging every child to build relationships.

Making inclusion work

Inclusion will only be successful when the school, parents and the local community are committed to making it a central focus for all policies and procedures. A shared belief in inclusion is paramount to success:

Inclusion is about change
It is not about changing the shape of the child (the square peg) so that it will fit into the round hole of the pegboard (the class) but about changing the shape of the round hole so that it supports the child.

This book will help teachers to identify and remove barriers experienced by children who are in mainstream schools and have special educational needs or disabilities. It is important to note that this book does not set out specifically to address the needs of children who have diagnosed syndromes such as 'Down's syndrome' or 'Di George syndrome'. Nor does it address the specific needs of children with visual, physical or hearing impairments. These are conditions that are largely medical in nature and it is acknowledged that many of these conditions can contribute to a range of learning difficulties. Some of the strategies outlined in this book may be helpful to teachers working with children having 'diagnosed' medical conditions. Where inclusion is fully embraced, all children will be able to participate, belong, achieve and be fully included in their class and school community.

In March 2011, the government published the SEN and Disability Green Paper which proposed a new approach to special educational needs and disability. They intend to develop a radically different system that will support better life outcomes for young people. Any legislative changes are to be taken forward from May 2012.

The Green Paper offers a visual representation of the main themes of the recommendations put forward by the government in the form of a 'word cloud'. In the illustration below, the larger the word, the more heavily it features in the Green Paper:

http://www.education.gov.uk/childrenandyoungpeople/sen/sen/a0075340/sen-and-disability-green-paper-word-cloud

The chapters of the Green Paper are:

1. Early identification and support
2. Giving parents control
3. Learning and achieving
4. Preparing for adulthood and
5. Services working together for families

The Green Paper acknowledges the importance of 'Identifying children's support needs early is vital if they are to thrive, and enables parents and professionals to put the right approach in place quickly' (Department for Education and Skills 2011. Support and aspiration: A new approach to special educational needs and disability. Para 11).

The Green Paper states the following:

● Teachers and other staff in schools and colleges are well trained and confident to: identify and overcome a range of barriers to learning; manage challenging behaviour; address bullying; and intervene early when problems emerge;

● Schools will have additional flexibility to support the needs of all pupils, and will have additional funding to support disadvantaged pupils through the pupil premium;

● Teachers feel able to identify effectively what a child needs to help them to learn and to plan support to help every child progress well, reflecting the specific needs of children with SEN and those who may just be struggling with learning and need school-based catch-up support which is normally available;

● Parents have the information they need about how the school is supporting their child; (Department for Education and Skills 2011. Support and aspiration: A new approach to special educational needs and disability. Para 23).

A Square Peg in a Round Hole embraces the vision of the Green Paper. It aims to help teachers to develop their skills in the identification of children with Special Educational Needs and to provide successful interventions. The book is an extremely useful training tool for student teachers, Newly Qualified Teachers (NQTs), experienced classroom teachers, SEN coordinators and head teachers.

1 Identifying reasons for differences in behaviour

Within any class of children, there will be several who present 'difference' in their behaviour. It is imperative that teachers look more closely at the behaviour being presented and find out the cause rather than making assumptions that the behaviour is deliberate or intentional. Children naturally want acceptance and seek to please adults. So when children demonstrate 'different' behaviour (some of which might be challenging) it is probable that there will be an underpinning reason for this behaviour. Rather than focusing on the behaviour, teachers need to determine the cause.

Factors influencing behaviour can include any of the following:

Additional needs

- Medical
- Educational

Language

- Difficulty
- Difference (English as an additional language)

Emotional and social

- Home environment
- Personal circumstances
- Well being

Cultural background

Unreasonable expectations

- Home
- School

Identifying reasons for differences in behaviour

It is vital that teachers actively assess – through observation and discussion with parents and colleagues – in order to identify what is underpinning the behaviour. Teachers can use the information from their own observations and discussions and reference them against the behaviours from the *Initial Framework of Reference* (below) in order to establish possible causes of the behaviour.

Areas of need

This framework outlines the following behaviours and difficulties associated with the following areas of need:

- Speech, language and communication

    o Receptive language

    o Expressive language

    o Reluctant speakers

    o Speech difficulties

- Autistic Spectrum Disorder

- Reading, writing, spelling and maths

    o Dyslexia

    o Dyscalculia

    o Dysgraphia

- Developmental Coordination Disorder (DCD)/dyspraxia

- Attention Deficit (Hyperactivity) Disorder (AD(H)D)

The list of behaviours or difficulties outlined in the *Initial Framework of Reference* is not a definitive list. The *Framework* is not intended to be used as a checklist but can be used to support the early identification and intervention process. Use your knowledge of the child to highlight the observed difficulties/behaviours that most accurately describe the child.

Identifying reasons for differences in behaviour

The Initial Framework of Reference (pages 14–21 and on the CD-ROM) describes behaviours or difficulties that a child may present. In order to highlight a behaviour, practitioners should have observed the child consistently over time. The framework focuses on five areas of need. The behaviours listed are most commonly associated with that specific area. However, you should be aware that children may not present all behaviours in each specific area and that behaviours you observe may fall into more than one area of need.

How to use the *Initial Framework of Reference*

Following your observations and discussions with parents and other adults who interact with the child, you may be able to highlight (on your print-outs) behaviours in one particular area thereby determining the specific area of need. It is important to consider whether or not the same behaviours or difficulties you have observed are also described in another area of need. For example, a child who has the *'inability to understand complex sentences'* (receptive language area) may also demonstrate *'language difficulties,'* associated with autism. Therefore, there may be a range of highlighted behaviours or difficulties across several areas of need. Where this occurs, focus on the area of need with the greatest number of behaviours highlighted. In all specific areas (apart from AD(H)D, reading, spelling and maths) the behaviours mostly commonly associated with that need are ranked in order.

If the first five behaviours/difficulties are highlighted, this would indicate a need for intervention. For AD(H)D, reading, spelling and maths, it is likely that most or all of the behaviours/difficulties will be highlighted. Where a sufficient number of behaviours/difficulties have been highlighted, the *SEN Code of Practice* procedure should then be initiated and intervention strategies implemented. To support the successful inclusion of the child within the classroom and school community, the appropriate chapter in this book will provide detailed information and will develop your understanding of how to remove the barriers to learning. Each chapter – colour-coded for ease of identification – contains strategies and advice to support you in successfully meeting the child's needs.

Identifying reasons for differences in behaviour

Initial framework of reference (also included in the CD-ROM)

1. Speech, language and communication

The following behaviours and difficulties may be observed:

Receptive language

- Inability or refusal to follow verbal instructions.

- Not seeming to listen when spoken to.

- Inability to understand complicated sentences.

- Giving the wrong response to questions.

- Parroting words or phrases (echolalia).

- Lack of interest when story books are read to them.

- Immature language (skills below the expected level for their age).

- Behavioural difficulties.

- Attention and listening difficulties.

- Quiet and withdrawn.

Expressive language

- Frequently having trouble finding the right word.

- Making grammatical mistakes and using poor sentence structure.

- Using the wrong words in sentences or confusing meaning in sentences.

- Mis-naming items.

- Relying on short, simple sentence construction.

- Inability to 'come to the point' or talking in circles.

- Problems with re-telling a story or relaying information.

- Inability to start or hold a conversation.

- Difficulty with oral and written work.

Identifying reasons for differences in behaviour

Reluctant speakers

Some children may be reluctant to speak for a number of reasons. This may be because English is not their first language or because they are electing not to speak, which is more common in very young children – perhaps in the first weeks of starting school. Reluctant speakers will go through a silent period and the transition from silence to speech will depend on the child and how the adult manages the transition. These children should not be considered for any specific interventions.

Speech difficulties

- Poor articulation of phonemes and words.*

- Omission of initial and final phonemes.*

- Slurred speech.

- Substitute certain letter sounds e.g. gog for dog, tar for car.

- Substitution of phonemes – initial, medial or final.*

- Dysfluency (stammer).

- Very limited or no speech.

- Reluctance to speak.

- May salivate excessively (younger children).

* These difficulties may be linked to an early or current hearing difficulty. A referral to a GP and/or speech and language therapist might be considered.

Glue ear is extremely common in young children. Children who are prone to frequent ear infections or a runny nose may experience intermittent hearing loss. This can fluctuate from day to day and can significantly affect a child's ability to hear and copy sounds accurately in speech.

Identifying reasons for differences in behaviour

2. Autistic Spectrum Disorder

The following behaviours and difficulties may be observed and may vary in severity from mild to severe.

- Lack of desire to communicate and limited or no eye contact.

- Inappropriate social behaviour.

- Demonstrates solitary play and lack of imagination.

- Demonstrates extreme behaviour.

- Demonstrates anxiety around or resists changes to routines or activities.

- Displays repetitive behaviour, e.g. hand flapping.

- Appears aloof or withdrawn.

- Repeats phrase, echolalic.

- Adopts alternative accents, e.g. American.

- Insists on sameness.

- Language difficulties.

- Can demonstrate aggression and/or self-injury when distressed or anxious.

- Can fixate on objects or a particular child.

- Demonstrates all-consuming focused interest, e.g. trains, vacuum cleaners, wheels, lights, etc.

- Seeks self-stimulating, repetitive activity e.g. banging, rocking, pacing, spinning, etc.

- Resists physical contact, e.g. hand holding.

- Over-sensitivity or under-sensitivity to pain.

- Over-sensitivity or under-sensitivity to sound, e.g. hands over ears.

- Over-sensitivity or under-sensitivity to touch, e.g. labels on clothes.

- Over-sensitivity or under-sensitivity to smell.

- Poor motor skills.

- Non-responsive to verbal cues.

Identifying reasons for differences in behaviour

Asperger's Syndrome

The following behaviours and difficulties may be observed:

- Difficulties with change demonstrated by mild to extreme reaction.

- Preoccupied with a particular subject of interest.

- Use of precise, literal language.

- Difficulty reading non-verbal cues (body language).

- Fixed agenda – finds it difficult or unwilling to adapt.

- Inappropriate social use of language and interactions.

- Misunderstanding of social rules, e.g. turn taking, compromising.

- Obsessional – likes things ordered, familiar, consistent.

- Can be rude and intolerant – can sometimes be described as 'spoilt' or wanting their own way.

- Prefers own company – will only seek engagement with others for own benefit.

- Clumsy and uncoordinated body movements.

- Bothered by sounds no one else seems to hear.

- Light sensitive.

- Tactile sensitivities.

- Prefers routine.

- Eating difficulties, e.g. will only eat certain foods.

- Poor motor skills.

- Adopts alternative accents, e.g. American.

- Uses high pitched 'sing-songy' voice (usually younger children).

3. Difficulties with reading, spelling, writing and maths (dyslexia, dyscalculia and dysgraphia)

The following behaviours and difficulties may be observed:

Reading, writing and spelling

- May have difficulty remembering what is heard in sequence.

- Poor auditory memory.

- Not be able to identify sounds, e.g. rhymes, syllables (phonological awareness).

- Poor phoneme/grapheme correspondence.

- Difficulty in ordering letters, days, months, etc.

- Slow reading speed and/or poor fluency.

- Difficulties in oral blending and segmenting.

- Spelling difficulties, e.g. reversals, substitutions, presenting phonetically plausible attempts.

- Poor visual memory.

- Inability to use written language to express thoughts.

Maths

- Difficulty in reciting the number words in the correct order.

- Poor auditory memory.

- Inability to count a number of objects accurately and consistently.

- Difficulties with reading and writing numerals.

- Inability to understand that a number is a symbol that represents a value.

- Difficulty in placing numbers in order of size.

- Difficulty with number facts, numerical procedures (counting on to add, counting back to subtract).

- Difficulty with principles, concepts and laws of arithmetic – understanding that addition is cumulative and subtraction is not.

4. Developmental coordination difficulties (DCD, dyspraxia)

The following behaviours and difficulties may be observed:

Pre-school

- Has difficulty with fine or gross fine motor skills.

- Trips and often bumps into things.

- Has difficulty negotiating space.

- Very high levels of motor activity, including feet swinging and tapping when seated, hand-clapping or twisting. Unable to stay still.

- High levels of excitability, with a loud/shrill voice.

- May be easily distressed and prone to temper tantrums.

- Hands flap when running.

- Difficulty with pedalling a tricycle or similar toy.

- Lack of any sense of danger (jumping from heights, etc.).

- Continued messy eating. May prefer to eat with fingers, frequently spills drinks.

- Avoidance of constructional toys, such as jigsaws or building blocks.

- Difficulty in holding a pencil or using scissors. Drawings may appear immature.

- Limited imaginative or creative play. May show little interest in dressing up or in playing appropriately in a home corner or play house.

- Isolation within the peer group. Rejected by peers – may prefer adult company.

- Laterality (left- or right-handedness) still not established.

- Persistent language difficulties.

- Sensitive to sensory stimulation, including high levels of noise, tactile defensiveness, wearing new clothes.

- Limited response to verbal instruction. May be slow to respond and have problems with comprehension.

- Limited concentration. Tasks are often left unfinished.

Identifying reasons for differences in behaviour

By age 7

- Slow completion of class work.

- Difficulties in adapting to a structured school routine.

- Difficulties in P.E. lessons.

- Slow at dressing. Unable to tie shoe laces.

- Barely legible handwriting.

- Immature drawing and copying skills.

- Limited concentration and poor listening skills.

- Literal use of language.

- Inability to remember more than two or three instructions at once.

- Continued high levels of motor activity.

- Hand flapping or clapping when excited.

- Tendency to become easily distressed and emotional.

- Problems with coordinating a knife and fork.

- Inability to form relationships with other children.

- Sleeping difficulties, including wakefulness at night and nightmares.

- Reporting of physical symptoms, such as migraine, headaches, feeling sick.

5. Attention Deficit (Hyperactivity) Disorder (AD(H)D)

The following behaviours and difficulties may be observed:

- Inattentive, easily distracted.
- Forgetful and disorganised.
- Restless, fidgety, always 'on the go'.
- Impulsive behaviour.
- Finds it difficult to manage their own behaviour.
- Unaware of danger.
- Blurts out answers to questions.
- Rarely completes work.
- Difficulty in following rules.
- Failing to finish tasks or sustain attention.
- Avoiding tasks that require sustained mental effort.
- Losing implements like pens or books.

Attention Deficit Disorder without the Hyperactivity (ADD) is less common but is present in some children:

- Limited attention and concentration.
- Quite passive.
- Appears to daydream.
- Rarely finishes tasks.
- Forgetful and disorganised.

Identifying reasons for differences in behaviour

▭ The impact of Special Educational Needs on a child's emotional well being

We haven't included a separate chapter on dealing with children's emotional well-being but it is important to consider the *emotional* impact of the difficulties experienced by children with Special Educational Needs who often require a great deal of emotional support both at home and at school.

You may observe some of the following behaviour/attitudes/actions which indicate that the child's emotional needs are not being met:

- Low self-esteem.

- Poor self-confidence.

- Looking sad and unhappy.

- Difficulty listening and concentrating with purpose.

- Easily distracted.

- Tendency to daydream.

- Reluctance to seek help or advice.

- Claiming not to 'understand'.

- Developing 'avoidance' tactics.

- Difficulty in making friends.

- Self harm.

- Showing aggression to peers.

Once teachers have adapted their expectations for that particular child and have put appropriate strategies into place to support the child's identified special needs, many of the emotional barriers mentioned above which are stumbling blocks to learning will be counteracted. The doorway for the child to progress, achieve and enjoy life within the school community will be opened wide.

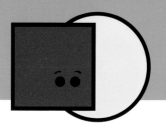
Effective Communication

Communication is all about how we interact with others, both verbally and non-verbally. It involves the skills necessary to convey ideas, concepts and thoughts. It relies on the use of language to question, to clarify, to describe and to discuss aspects of the world around us as well as our internal thoughts and feelings. Communication relies on the skills of conversation – knowing how to talk to others, how to take turns, how to change the type of language we use to suit the situation or the person being spoken to. It also depends on the ability to interpret and respond to other people's thoughts and ideas.

As well as making use of spoken language, effective communication is also non-verbal. Eye contact, body posture, gesture, facial expression displaying interest/surprise/boredom, etc. can be just as expressive as words. If the two strands of verbal and non-verbal communication are in conflict with each other, then we give mixed messages to the people with whom we are attempting to communicate. If children arrive in the classroom without the ability to communicate effectively, then they will be disadvantaged from the outset and will experience difficulty accessing the curriculum. They will not be able to convey what they do and don't know or understand, what they like or dislike.

'There is a group of children who are starting school with SLCN poor language skills; inadequate for starting formal learning. These children may have a small vocabulary, be just starting to join words together, find it hard to listen and may sound like a much younger child. With the right support, they may catch up with their peers. In some areas, particularly areas of social disadvantage, this group may be upwards of 50% of children at school entry.'
(I CAN Talk Series: Issue 7 Speech, Language and Communication Needs and the Early Years)

Speech, language and communication

A number of reasons are given for this decline in children's early communication skills:

Forward-facing buggies

It's difficult to push and talk to a child when the child is facing away from the person pushing the buggy. Without stopping and going around to the front of the buggy it's impossible to have eye contact or engage in a running commentary on the sights, sounds and smells encountered along the way.

New technology

- Parents have been observed pushing buggies listening to music with headphones or talking on their mobile phones, oblivious to their infants' crying. Parents sometimes become isolated in their own world, leaving the child to become isolated in their world.

- More time is being spent watching television. Channels such as CBBC are transmitting for longer periods of time. Sometimes children are strapped into chairs and placed in front of a television screen to keep them occupied and quiet. They are receiving aural and visual stimulation but it's all one way. Communication is a two way process.

DVDs, computers and games consoles

Needless to say, these have their value but they tend to encourage children to become more isolated. Children are occupied with little need to communicate. Their mental activity is dominated by the actions and dramas provided by the games rather than developing their own independent imagination and thoughts.

Mealtimes

Increasingly, families are not eating a meal together round a table. The opportunities to communicate together as a family are lost as children's attention is drawn to other distractions such as the television, or a meal is eaten in isolation or away from the parents.

Central heating

Back in the 'good old days', families needed to huddle together in the one room which was heated by a fire. They had to spend time together and had regular opportunities for conversation. Parents and children now spend more time in separate rooms. Even though the television can draw children and parents together into the same room, there is often little opportunity to discuss what has been watched or even what has taken place during the day.

Many children are entering primary school without the speech, language and communication (SLC) skills they need to learn, to make friends and to achieve. Those who have not developed these good SLC skills will find it hard to express themselves, understand instructions and speak in sentences. They will find it difficult to access the curriculum and are likely to experience difficulties with reading, writing and spelling. In order to learn, children need to have good speaking, listening and communication skills and an appropriate vocabulary. Lack of language skills will impact on both their social and emotional development.

Teachers within schools and early years settings have a very important role in identifying when a child might have SLC needs. The National Strategies Inclusion Development Programme 'Supporting children with speech, language and communication needs' provides practical advice on early identification of these needs.

Children having other identified special needs, such as specific learning difficulties (dyslexia, dyscalculia, etc.), Autistic Spectrum Disorders and social emotional behavioural difficulties (AD(H)D), may also have significant speech, language and communication difficulties.

'In order to progress to become competent readers and writers, children need to have developed good speech, language and communication skills. They need to be able to understand – to comprehend – language, as well as developing the skills to use language to express themselves. Children need to have well developed vocabularies, with a real depth of understanding of the meanings of words. Most children will do this using oral language, but some children may need to use augmentative methods of communication, such as signing.' (National Strategies 2008. Inclusion Development Programme: Supporting children with speech, language and communication needs: Guidance for practitioners in the Early Years Foundation Stage. Nottingham: DCSF, page 8)

Speech, language and communication

🔲 Speech, language and communication difficulties

The range of speech, language and communication (SLC) difficulties children experience can be categorised under the following four main headings:

Pragmatic difficulties
Social skills

Speech sound difficulties
Selecting sounds
Articulating sounds
Phonological awareness

Receptive language difficulties
Concepts
Vocabulary
Sentence structure

Expressive language difficulties
Sequencing
Word finding
Auditory memory
Using grammar

Pragmatic difficulties

– the use of language in a social context.

- Difficulty in responding to instructions correctly due to misinterpretations.

- Difficulty in understanding the meaning of words.

- Difficulty in understanding and responding to words linked to emotions, such as 'embarrassed' or 'anxious'.

- Will often take things literally e.g. 'I can't spend time, but I can spend money' (10 year old).

- May suddenly change the subject due to lack of understanding of the key topic of conversation.

Speech sound difficulties

- Sounds not articulated accurately.

- Not having the means to communicate verbally using sounds.

- Not speaking fluently.

- Not being able to speak with expression, with a clear voice, using pitch, volume and intonation to support meaning.

Speech, language and communication

Receptive language difficulties

- Difficulty in understanding spoken language.
- Difficulty in learning new vocabulary.
- The inability to process information and respond appropriately.
- Misinterpretation of verbal instructions.
- Inability to remember or hold a series of instructions.
- Difficulty in understanding and interpreting what people say.

Expressive language difficulties

- Difficulty in expressing thoughts verbally.
- Thinking one word but saying another.
- Saying words in the wrong order.
- Beginning a sentence but unable to finish the sentence accurately.
- Difficulty using words to build up sentences, sentences to build up conversations and to narrate.

Children with SLC difficulties find listening and attending very challenging. We might assume that when children are not listening and paying attention, they are doing it with intent. Sitting on the carpet, listening to a story, is a challenge for a child who may have receptive language or pragmatic difficulties. If the activity does not have meaning or does not engage them, then they will often lose concentration and let their minds wander into their own world. This can lead to unacceptable behaviour and disruption to the activity. Some children need support in developing their listening and attention skills. We need to evaluate the methods used to communicate with children and consider developing alternative ways to engage them. By using visual and tangible aids e.g. story sacks, real objects, signs and symbols, etc., we can successfully develop the child's ability to listen, attend and participate in the activity.

Children who have SLC difficulties struggle to make their needs known. They are unable to tell others about their likes or dislikes. Relationships are based on communication but children who cannot understand or pronounce words will find it difficult to interact and communicate with others.

Teachers can support the inclusion of children with speech, language and communication needs by implementing the strategies on page 29.

Let Sophie tell you about her world. Sophie has speech and language difficulties and visits a speech and language therapist once a week.

Speech, language and communication

Sophie's story

Hi, my name is Sophie. I'm five years old and just about to move into Year 1. I love school. I like playing in the home corner.

I can speak but my words don't sound like everyone else. I can't say some words very well and it takes me a long time to make people understand what I'm saying. This really upsets me and sometimes I get really frustrated.

I don't like talking to my teacher when anyone else is there because I feel silly. I don't have many friends in my class so I play on my own. I don't mind because that means I don't have to speak much. My Mum understands me all the time, though, when I'm at home. I love my Mum.

Mrs Brown talks a lot. I often don't understand what she says and I have to guess sometimes. I used to get into trouble for not doing something. I want to do what she asks, but sometimes I just can't work out what she is saying and never know what is happening. I sometimes wait a while and watch what the other children are doing, then I copy them.

When I first started in Reception, Mrs Brown said that I never did as I was asked and she told my Mum. I didn't think she liked me as she thought I was naughty. My Mum explained that I didn't understand everything that people said and that I would need a bit of help. I used to cry for my Mum.

Now when Mrs Brown says something, she says it more slowly and doesn't use as many words. It's great because I can understand her a lot better. We have lots of pictures and things in my classroom. They help me know where things are and there are even pictures on a string like a washing line. It helps me to know what we are doing while I'm at school. I know what Mrs Brown wants me to do and when she wants me to do it so I don't feel silly. Mrs Parker who works in our room sometimes plays with me and asks Sarah and Molly to play too. They are my friends. I try to speak to them but when they don't understand I get Mrs Parker or Mrs Brown to help.

I go and visit Fiona once a week and we do fun games and things as well as a lot of talking. I like being with Fiona – she helps me to say my words properly and I'm learning more and more about words and I am beginning to understand what she's saying. I am learning to use a sign language called Makaton as well as using my talking. This is great as it makes everything so much easier. She said that we are going to teach it to the other boys and girls in my class. I can't wait.

My Mum and Mrs Brown have been learning Makaton with me. It's like our own special way of talking. Mrs Brown taught everyone a few signs today at carpet time. I feel really cool because I can do it better than anyone at the moment and everyone is beginning to understand me and I can understand them more easily if they use signs as well as talking.

I'm not so scared to talk any more.

⊂⊃ Suggested strategies

Receptive and expressive difficulties

- Develop the visual environment.

- Clearly label areas of the room with signs, pictures or symbols (see page 70 and CD-ROM).

- Display a class visual timetable (see page 71).

- Introduce visual/auditory prompts for gaining whole class attention and for giving whole group instructions.

- Convey meaning through pictures, photographs, modelling, demonstrating and running commentary.

- Always gain eye contact before giving information or instructions.

- Confirm understanding with the child.

- Provide structure for written work and support for recalling or re-telling.

- Use gesture and exaggerated facial expressions to accompany language.

- Keep language simple.

- Continuously model and extend language.

- Help children communicate with each other – adult support/play partner.

- Display visual behavioural prompts and expectations.

- Keep layout of the room unchanged.

- Purposefully plan seating to maximise eye contact.

- Anticipate situations that a child might find challenging and plan to support appropriately.

Reluctant speakers

- Continue talking even when the child does not respond.

- Be persistent in including them in small groups with other children.

- Use varied questions.

- Use other children as the focus in the conversation (pair the learner with a buddy and ask questions of both children).

- Accept non-verbal responses.

- Praise even minimal efforts.

- Continue to expect that the child will respond.

- Structure lessons to encourage child-to-child interaction.

- Provide activities which reinforce language practice through role-play.

- Introduce visual communication prompts to help the child indicate his/her intent.

- Acknowledge that a child may be an excellent communicator but may have unintelligible speech.

Speech difficulties

- Model correct speech.

- Provide child with prompts to indicate a response or request.

- Value and respond to the child's attempts to communicate both verbally and non-verbally.

- Maintain eye contact.

- Offer time and patience – WAIT.

Having read through the information on speech, language and communication needs and the strategies for providing appropriate support for children with SLC needs, turn to Chapter 7: The inclusive learning environment (page 67). This provides more specific information on developing an inclusive classroom. A list of suggested resources is provided after Chapter 7 on pages 76–79. The resources are colour-coded to match the colours for each area of need in this book.

3 Autistic Spectrum Disorder

📖 Autism

Children diagnosed with autism are often described as being on the 'autistic spectrum'. The term Autistic Spectrum Disorder (ASD) is used to refer to children diagnosed with autism and Asperger's Syndrome. These conditions share the same three areas of difficulty to a greater or larger extent. Some children with ASD will grow up to function with relatively little support, whilst others will need specialist support for life. ASD is a lifelong developmental disability which affects how a person communicates and relates to other people. Leo Kranner (Kranner 1943. Autistic disturbances of affective contact.) was the first person to identify a pattern of abnormal behaviour in young children. The term he used to describe these patterns of behaviour was 'early infantile autism' and the condition was considered to be rare. In 1979, Lorna Wing and Judith Gould examined the prevalence of autism amongst children diagnosed with special needs in the London borough of Camberwell. They used Kranner's definition and found that the prevalence of autism was 5 in 10,000. They then widened their definition to include children who displayed impairments of social interaction, communication and imagination and displayed repetitive stereotypical patterns of behaviour. They found that the total prevalence rate for children identified as being within the broader autism spectrum was approximately 20 in every 10,000 children (Wing and Gould 1979. Severe impairments of social interaction and associated abnormailities in children).

The National Autistic Society currently estimates that there could be over 500,000 people who have an ASD. This prevalence rate of around 1 in 100 is a best estimate of the prevalence in children (National Autistic Society 2010. Statistics: How many people have people have Autism Spectrum Disorder). Males are four times more likely to have ASD than females. There is a general assumption that the rate of autism has risen over the last 20 years. This is in fact not the case – it is the definition of autism that has broadened. Within this time frame, the inclusion of children with special educational needs and disability has become the norm within mainstream schools.

Autistic Spectrum Disorder

What do we know about autism?

Children with autism experience a triad of impairment:

- Social communication
- Social interaction
- Social imagination

Social communication

Children with autism find it difficult to interpret all forms of non-verbal communication:

- Gestures
- Facial expression
- Eye contact
- Body language
- Posture
- Touch

When we consider that a large percentage of our communication is non-verbal, we begin to realise how difficult it is for a child with autism to function within the world. They find it difficult to know how to start a conversation. Then, they may not know how to finish a conversation. In conversation, they can use complex words and phrases that they have heard but the meaning of which they do not understand. Children with autism often take language literally. For example, a child when asked to run on the spot in a P.E. lesson will go looking for 'a spot'. In conversation, they 'say it as it is' e.g. they may call another child 'fat'. When asked by an adult 'Why are you calling them names?' they will respond by saying 'Because she is'. They will not understand that this is socially inappropriate or react to the emotional response the other child displays. Humour and sarcasm are often beyond their understanding and when children are laughing around them they are unresponsive.

Autistic Spectrum Disorder

Social interaction

A child with autism may often be isolated. They want to have friends and be sociable but lack the understanding about how to make friends and keep them. They attempt to interact with their peers but because they don't understand social rules, they may stand too close, stare into their face, follow them around or start a conversation that may be of no interest to the other child.

They misinterpret the behaviour and reactions of others and often find it confusing or they may copy the behaviour assuming it is the right way to behave. Alternatively, they may not respond to others or even demonstrate a complete lack of interest, appearing aloof. The difficulty they have in responding and conforming to socially acceptable behaviour can prevent them from being accepted and understood by others. They can appear to demonstrate little regard for social expectation and do not conform to expected 'rules'. During a whole class discussion, the child with autism may interrupt and talk continuously about something that is unrelated to the class discussion and when reminded of the 'rules', they continue their monologue.

Social imagination

Some children with autism will appear to be highly imaginative through a special interest and may demonstrate a high level of skill as a musician, photographer, artist or writer.

A child with autism finds it difficult to see beyond what is factual or literal. They are unable to make predictions, regardless of cues or clues that are available to them. They prefer to work or play in a logical and systematic way. If presented with resources that could be used in an imaginative way, they tend to use the resources in rigid, structured ways, e.g. when playing with cars they won't pretend they are going on a journey but rather they will line the cars up in a rigid and systematic way. They can be high achievers in maths as they prefer the logical and systematic content of the subject.

Children with autism experience the world in a different way from most other children. They find it difficult to talk and express themselves using words. They need support to be able to communicate.

Their response to the world around them is different from other children. This is because their senses are heightened. Their reaction to sound, touch, taste and smell can be extreme. They may cover their ears in response to loud noises or they may not react at all to a sound or they may create constant noise. They can be resistant to gentle touch and attempt to move away or they don't seem to notice the touch of others. Some children with autism cannot differentiate between hot and cold, loud and quiet, hard and soft. Their reaction to textures in foods, furniture or textiles can be negative. Activities that involve touching materials such as clay, paint or water will be avoided.

Autistic Spectrum Disorder

Some children may walk close to walls. Their body posture may be rigid, they may move constantly, they may rock or walk in circles. Food can be an issue as some children with autism seem to want food constantly whilst others may gag when eating or refuse to eat altogether. They may lick, chew or smell objects in the environment. A child with autism finds it difficult to cope in environments that are visually or auditorily over-stimulating. Their behaviour can appear irrational and uncontrollable. The reason for this response is that their brain is experiencing sensory overload. A child with autism may attempt to escape from the sensory overload. They may try and run out of the room or hide under a table – seeking a place of comfort and reduced sensory stimulation.

Wendy Lawson, an adult with high functioning autism, wrote, 'As a child growing up I was expected to "play" with other children. For me, the difficulty was that I didn't have a concept of what play was or why it was considered to be fun. Most children's play made no sense to me.'

She wrote the following poem:

What is Play?

'Wendy, Wendy,' I hear the teacher say.
'Wendy, Wendy,' please look this way.
'Wendy, Wendy,' I hear the children say.
'Wendy, Wendy,' please come and play.

I hear the words that come each day.
'What do they mean?' I hear me say.
Words without pictures simply go away.
I turn my head and look instead
At all that glitters; blue, green and red.

'You'll like it here,' Father speaks,
'Come and play with Billy.'
Inside my head my brain just freaks,
'How can they be so silly?'

'Why would I want to do this thing?'
My mind can find no reason.
'Please leave me with the sparkly string.
This gives me such a feeling.'

(Lawson 2006)

Autistic Spectrum Disorder

◻) Asperger's Syndrome

The condition was first identified in 1944 by Hans Asperger, a Viennese paediatrician. His research identified a pattern of behaviour and abilities – predominantly amongst boys – including a lack of empathy, impaired imagination, difficulty in making friends, obsession in a special interest and often problems with motor coordination.

A child who has a diagnosis of Asperger's Syndrome is on the autistic spectrum – it is a form of autism. It is a lifelong disability; however, focused interventions can have a significant impact on how the individual functions within and makes sense of the world.

A child with Asperger's will have difficulties in all three areas of impairment: social communication, social interaction and social imagination. The degree to which they experience these difficulties is different from that of a child on the autistic spectrum. They will not have experienced delayed language development when younger; in fact their language can be described as 'sophisticated'. A child with Asperger's is often described as 'high functioning', i.e. they often have above-average intelligence. They can skilfully articulate their knowledge and understanding about a personal, focused interest (or fascination). For example, a young child who has a focused interest in dinosaurs will often be able to share an in-depth knowledge of this topic, far beyond what would be expected of a child of that age.

What makes the child with Asperger's different?

- They will have a special, focused interest.
- They will have a need for routines and familiarity.
- They will interpret words and actions literally.
- They will have difficulty in making and sustaining friendships.
- They do not always conform.
- They are unable to respond to the emotions of others.

How do children with Asperger's manage these difficulties?

Children with Asperger's, depending on their age, will present a wide range of behavioural differences. Because of their level of intelligence, as these children mature they begin to self-manage and develop strategies to deal with the issues they have around this triad of impairment.

Consider, for example a child that will only use a red coloured pencil for mark making or writing. When a red pencil is not available, depending on their age, these may be the responses at different stages of self-management:

- A very young child who has not yet been diagnosed will often become very distressed, angry and/or throw a temper tantrum and will refuse to use any other pencil. This may be interpreted as stubbornness, attention seeking or a general 'tantrum'. The reason for this is that the child associates the red pencil with 'mark making' activities and creates a visual image of this function (e.g. red pencil = mark making, mark making = red pencil), and finds it impossible to change the visual image they have created for themselves. Consequently they cannot do the mark-making activity without the red pencil.

- A slightly older child, who realises that they need to use a red pencil, may ask the teacher or go in search of a red pencil. If the teacher doesn't find a red pencil, the child may still become very anxious and/or distressed and refuse to comply. This reaction can be seen as disruptive and not age-appropriate behaviour and can be viewed as the child simply 'wanting their own way'.

- When a child is beginning to develop self-managing strategies, they, or someone in school, will anticipate this situation. They may try to resolve this difficulty by themselves. They may ask the teacher for a red pencil, or may get up without asking to find one from somewhere else. If the child has anticipated this situation in advance, they may have a red pencil in their pocket or bag or may have one in their tray. It may be that their mum (who knows the child's individual preferences) has anticipated this difficulty and has provided them with their own red pencil.

Children with Asperger's are often diagnosed later than children with autism. This is because the syndrome varies from child to child. The difficulties the child is experiencing may not be recognised in early childhood and they may not be given a diagnosis of Asperger's until late childhood or adulthood.

Autistic Spectrum Disorder

As teachers, it would be very helpful if we could see through the eyes of a child with Asperger's. Children may arrive in school having experienced a range of situations or challenges. Any of these can greatly affect how they cope with the day ahead. We need to understand how they think and feel and respond to everyday events. They view the world and interpret social situations in a very different way from many other children.

Teachers can support the inclusion of children with an Autistic Spectrum Disorder by implementing the strategies on page 39.

Let Luke tell you about his world. Luke has been diagnosed with Asperger's Syndrome:

Luke's story

Hi, my name is Luke. I am nine years old. I have Asperger's Syndrome. This makes me quite different from other children. I don't have friends because other children prefer not to play with me. I'm a bit bossy and I don't like to share anything. When I get something, I have to keep it and when I see something I have to have it. Other children don't like this. Sometimes if I need some help I will ask another child to do it but when they have finished, I don't want to play with them any more.

I get very involved in what I'm doing and don't want to stop. My teachers ask me to stop and tidy up but this upsets and worries me as I don't want to stop and do something else. I become very agitated when this happens and sometimes scream and cry. That's because I feel a bit scared as I'm not sure what is going to happen next.

I had a bad day today. It started out bad because my Mum didn't have my clothes laid out for me on my bed. When she did put them out she laid out my yellow jumper and not my green one. I didn't want to wear my yellow one but Mum didn't know this. I got quite angry and had a bit of a strop and threw my yellow jumper on the floor. Mum knows me quite well and realised that I probably wanted to wear a different colour jumper so she got a blue one and a green one for me to choose. I chose the green one and I was happy.

I had two Weetabix for breakfast with just a little milk. I don't like a lot of milk as it makes the Weetabix go soggy. I had my red bowl and red spoon and had orange juice in my red cup. I spilt a drop of milk on my green jumper. I didn't like this. Mum tried to wipe it off but I could still see the mark it left. My Mum scrubbed hard and it eventually came off. I was happy again.

Time for school. All my school things were ready for me by the door. Uh-oh…it was raining! I don't like the rain because I have to wear a hat and I hate that. I didn't wear it and so I got my hair all wet. I protested all the way to school because my hair was getting wet. My Mum did allow me to take my red colouring pencil with me.

I was in a bad mood when I got to school. My 'helper', Mrs Tringle, came to say hello but I didn't say hello back to her. Sometimes I do and sometimes I don't. I took off my coat and hung it on my peg. I went into the classroom and walked to the carpet. Jack was sitting where I usually sit. I didn't like this and asked him to move. He wouldn't so I shouted and screamed at him. Mrs Tringle came over and asked him to move.

Autistic Spectrum Disorder

Miss Stacey was talking to us about what we were going to do today and stuck picture cards on the string. She didn't put playtime on. Why didn't she put playtime on? I'll have to tell her.

'Miss Stacey, you haven't put playtime on. Why haven't you put playtime on? We always have playtime – it goes there, just after Literacy. Are you going to put it on? It needs to go on – there, right there. Shall I get it for you?'

Then Miss Stacey said, 'Well, today Luke we will be going into the hall for a special surprise. I'm going to put this question mark on the string instead. It's going to be fun.'

Oh dear, my day was not going to plan…and somebody was sitting on my red chair!

Suggested strategies

- Use gesture or real objects to convey meaning.

- Provide children with a visual daily routine: this will help them understand the structure of the day.

- Create choice boards.

- Be prepared to make adaptations to class routines to support individual needs.

- Give advance warnings of changes to routines or activities to support smooth transition.

- Provide visual organisational aids such as checklists or prompt sheets.

- Provide a computer for writing tasks.

- Provide a distraction-free area for children who need it, like a small screened-off space with a minimum of visual stimulation.

- Provide the child with their own easily identified designated space on the carpet area. Use a cushion or a mat. For older children, give the child their own named chair.

- Consider providing a system to support the child's participation in an activity from beginning to end, for example, start box – task – finish box – reward.

- Use sand timers to help the child keep on task or to wait.

- Maintain consistency and familiarity for the child.

- Ensure that all staff have the same expectations of the child.

- Use the child's name (then wait ten seconds for the child to respond) or use a visual cue to focus the child's attention before communicating.

- Use visual symbols, photographs or objects to support the child's understanding.

- Break down instructions on how to complete a task into steps. The instructions can either be presented in a visual or written form. For example, the child selects the first instruction. When they have completed this, they then select the next instruction.

- Use the child's special interest or 'fascination' as a vehicle for learning.

- Allow the child free access to their 'fiddle object'.

- Use the child's special interest as a vehicle for learning concepts and skills for teaching turn taking.

- Use simple language alongside visual cues.

- When communicating, ask direct questions – say what you mean, mean what you say.

- Don't insist on the child making eye contact. Try standing side to side when communicating.

- Provide a quiet area where the child can go when they are feeling anxious or distressed. Placing a cherished object, e.g. a glitter stick, for the child to fiddle with in this area will comfort the child.

- Ignore behaviour that does not adversely affect the working atmosphere of the classroom.

- Use 'Social Stories'. These can be used to teach social skills and the rules of social conduct.

What to avoid

- Over-stimulating classroom walls and hanging resources.

- Bold primary colours – consider using natural and pastel colours.

- Loud background noise.

- Scented oils, perfume, etc.

- Prolonged carpet time or sitting for too long.

- Making unnecessary or sudden changes.

- Using metaphorical speech, such as 'Wait a minute'.

- Asking 'why' questions.

- Raising your voice or shouting across the classroom.

- Confrontation, where possible.

Having read through the information on Autistic Spectrum Disorder and the strategies for providing appropriate support for children with ASD, turn to Chapter 7: The inclusive learning environment (page 67). This provides more specific information on developing an inclusive classroom. A list of suggested resources is provided on pages 77–79. The resources are colour-coded to match the colours for each area of need in this book.

4 Difficulties with reading, writing, spelling and maths

Specific Learning Difficulties

The term Specific Learning Difficulties (SpLD) is frequently used within the education community to describe children who mainly have a difficulty with reading, writing, spelling and maths, although it is now widely accepted that a number of other areas, including memory, organisation and concentration, can be affected.

Dyslexia, rather than the term Specific Learning Difficulties (SpLD), is now being used consistently in government documentation to describe a specific difficulty in learning to read. In May 2008 the secretary of state invited Jim Rose to undertake a review of dyslexia. The National Strategies subsequently published *The Inclusion Development Programme (IDP): Dyslexia and speech, language and communications needs (SLCN).*

Dyscalculia, rather than the term Specific Learning Difficulties (SpLD), is used to describe a specific difficulty with numbers and arithmetic. Dyscalculia was formally recognised as a specific learning disability by the DfES in 2001. They defined dyscalculia as:

'A condition that affects the ability to acquire arithmetical skills. Dyscalculic learners may have difficulty understanding simple number concepts, lack an intuitive grasp of numbers and have problems learning number facts and procedures. Even if they produce a correct answer or use a correct method, they may do so mechanically and without confidence'.

(Department for Education and Skills 2001, The National Numeracy Strategy: Guidance to support pupils with dyslexia and dyscalculia. Nottingham: DfES.)

Dysgraphia, rather than the term Specific Learning Difficulties (SpLD), is used to describe a specific difficulty with transferring ideas easily into written form. This means having severe problems with the written word, which is affected by extreme difficulty with fine motor skills.

Dyslexia

> *The term dyslexia is derived from two Greek words, 'dys' meaning difficulty and 'lexicos' meaning words. The literal meaning is therefore 'difficulty with words', or difficulty reading and spelling words.*

Jim Rose, in his independent report, defines dyslexia as a learning difficulty that primarily affects the skills involved in accurate and fluent word reading and spelling. He identifies the characteristic features of dyslexia as difficulties in phonological awareness, verbal memory and verbal processing speed. He acknowledges that dyslexia occurs across the range of intellectual abilities. There is evidence that children with dyslexia may have 'co-occurring' factors or difficulties. These may be seen in aspects of language, motor coordination, mental calculation, concentration and personal organisation, but these are not, by themselves, markers of dyslexia.

Difficulties with reading, writing, spelling and maths

The table below summarises the common features of dyslexia-related literacy difficulties observed during childhood, adolescence and adulthood.

Developmental phases of dyslexia in children and young people learning to read English

Developmental phase	Signs of dyslexia
Pre-school	Delayed or problematic speech. Poor expressive language. Poor rhyming skills. Little interest/difficulty learning letters.
Early school years	Poor letter-sound knowledge. Poor phoneme awareness. Poor word attack skills. Idiosyncratic spelling. Problems copying.
Middle school years	Slow reading. Poor decoding skills when faced with new words. Phonetic or non-phonetic spelling.
Adolescence and adulthood	Poor reading fluency. Slow speed of writing. Poor organisation and expression in work.

Rose 2009. Identifying and teaching children and young people with dyslexia and literacy difficulties: An independent report from Sir Jim Rose to the Secretary of State for Children, Schools and Families. Nottinghamshire: HMSO page 32).

Some children with dyslexia may experience difficulty with maths. This may be because they misunderstand the wording of a mathematical question rather than with the number concepts involved in solving the problem.

They may also experience the following difficulties:

● Confusion with place value.

● Remembering sequences – tables, months, days, dates.

● The concept of time, e.g. yesterday, today, tomorrow.

Difficulties with reading, writing, spelling and maths

- Telling the time and time awareness (use of timetables, organisation, etc. – may also suffer as a result of poor personal organisation skills).

- Number and symbol reversals.

- Confusion of symbols such as + and x signs.

- Learning and remembering multiplication tables.

'Dyslexia is a learning 'difference" rather than a learning "difficulty". If they don't learn the way we teach them, we must teach them the way they learn.'

(Primary National Strategies 2005. Learning and teaching for dyslexic children. London: HMSO)

Let Rachel tell you about her world. Rachel is nine years old and has been diagnosed as having dyslexia.

Rachel's story

I always have trouble with reading and spelling. I have difficulty sounding out words – the words never fit together right. If I hear the word said first, then I can learn the word. I do best in classes like science when the material is spoken out loud by the teacher. I have a hard time understanding things because I have a hard time sounding out words. I get my letters jumbled up, like 'b' for 'd' and '96' for '69'. Spelling would be my best subject if I could memorize the words just before the test. Afterwards I forget the spellings and have to start all over again. I always make the same mistakes like spelling 'those' as 'thoughs' and anything with an 'f' sound incorrectly, like 'phone' as 'fone'. I can't spell 'spaghetti'. I have to use a dictionary to help me.

I'm not very confident. When under pressure, my spelling and reading get much worse. I get really embarrassed with my friends. I work so much harder than them. I feel silly and stupid and I always try to hide my work. However, I'm not teased by the kids in my class; in fact I have lots of friends. My Mum and Dad help me a lot at home too.

I listen a lot in class. I sometimes get a bit lost. It sometimes doesn't make any sense to me. I think that's why I have so much trouble in maths too – well, just about everything else, really. I love music and P.E. I do best in lessons when the teachers talk a lot and put work on the white board. I have a lot of trouble when I have to do the reading all on my own. I panic and freeze up.

I love ice skating. I go to a skating club after school and on a Saturday morning. I love it but I get frustrated. I'm left-handed and have problems with directions. When you learn how to skate, you learn to jump and spin in the same direction because you should be spinning in the same direction whether you are on the ground or in the air. Oh gosh! Did this take some learning! I can't spin and jump in the same direction. I jump in the wrong direction. I spin to the right all of the time. I wish I could spin to the left!

◁▷ Dyscalculia

> The term dyscalculia is derived from two Greek words, 'dys' meaning difficulty and 'calculia' meaning calculation. The literal meaning is therefore 'difficulty with numbers' or an inability to calculate.

Dyscalculia is used as a term to describe people who have an unexpected difficulty dealing with mathematical problems. There is little research on its nature and causes. Children with dyscalculia struggle with the most basic aspects of numbers and arithmetic, though many achieve good or even excellent levels in other areas of learning. Research suggests that dyscalculia is a Specific Learning Difficulty (SpLD) as is dyslexia.

Dyscalculia is thought to relate to problems in working memory and the inability to relate numbers as abstracts to absolute quantities. Children with dyscalculia may be helped by using visual/spatial cues and strategies, though understanding concepts of number and arithmetic will never be an easy task. A child with dyscalculia may struggle with some or all of the following activities in everyday life: telling the time, remembering phone numbers, calculating prices and handling change, measuring things such as temperature or speed.

Typical symptoms of dyscalculia

- Counting: Children with dyscalculia can usually learn the sequence of counting words but may have difficulty navigating back and forth, especially in twos and threes.

- Calculations: Children with dyscalculia find learning and recalling number facts difficult. They often lack confidence even when they produce the correct answer. They also find it difficult to use rules and procedures to build on known facts, e.g. they may know that $5 + 3 = 8$ but not realise that $3 + 5 = 8$ (reversal of numbers equals the same amount) and $5 + 4 = 9$ (increasing a number by one increases the answer by one).

- Numbers with zeros: Children with dyscalculia may find it difficult to grasp that the words ten, hundred and thousand have the same relationship to each other as the numerals 10, 100 and 1000.

- Measures: Children with dyscalculia often have difficulty with operations such as handling money or telling the time. They may also have problems with concepts such as speed (miles per hour) or temperature.

- Direction/orientation: Children with dyscalculia may have difficulty understanding spatial orientation (including left and right) causing difficulties in following directions or with map reading.

Children with dyscalculia may have difficulties where teachers follow an interactive, whole-class method of teaching. Asking children with dyscalculia to answer simple mathematical questions in public will inevitably lead to embarrassment and frustration. A multi-sensory approach to teaching mathematics is appropriate.

Dyscalculia and dyslexia occur both independently of each other and together. The strategies for dealing with dyscalculia will be fundamentally the same whether or not the learner is also dyslexic. Difficulty in decoding written words can transfer across into a difficulty in decoding mathematical notation and symbols. For some children with dyslexia, however, difficulty with mathematics may in fact stem from problems with the language surrounding mathematical questions rather than with number concepts, e.g. their dyslexia may cause them to misunderstand the wording of a question.

Dysgraphia

The term dysgraphia is derived from two Greek words *'dys' meaning difficulty and 'graphein' meaning to write. The literal meaning is therefore 'difficulty with handwriting' or an inability to form letters.*

A child with dysgraphia can have good oral language skills but will be unable to produce written letter forms by hand. They are unable to use written language to express their thoughts.

Typical symptoms of children with dysgraphia

Children may:

- Find it difficult to hold a pencil comfortably.
- Write slowly and laboriously.
- Have inconsistent letter formation and use a mixture of upper and lower case letters.
- Mix the order of letters in the middle of words, while getting the initial and final letters correct.
- Use a rubber excessively.
- Find it difficult to copy from a board.
- Write the wrong word or omit a word when trying to formulate words on paper.
- Have difficulty forming sentences or phrases and using grammatical rules to write sentences.
- Find it difficult to think and write at the same time.

Difficulties with reading, writing, spelling and maths

A child with dysgraphia will not be able to reflect their abilities in reading, speaking and listening in the content of their writing. It will be difficult to read the child's writing as letters may be of inconsistent size and poorly formed. Words may be spelt incorrectly and sentences will not make sense. When attempting to write they may experience pain and their posture will be poor. In addition, children with dysgraphia usually have some type of problem with working memory. They will find it difficult to remember the shape of letters, words and numbers.

Teachers can support the inclusion of children with reading, writing, spelling and maths difficulties by implementing the strategies on page 47.

Difficulties with reading, writing, spelling and maths

Suggested strategies

- Develop a visual learning environment.

  - Clearly lable storage containers.

  - Use picture prompts.

  - Devise a storage and retrieval system.

All photocopied reading material should be copied onto pastel-coloured paper.

Provide individual:

- Alphabet cards.

- Days of the week cards, etc.

- Grapheme cards.

- Word banks.

- Scribble pads.

- Whiteboards.

- Picture/word dictionaries.

- Handwriting models and mnemonics.

- Number grids.

- Number lines.

- Digit symbols.

- Number fans.

- Number strips.

- Maths dictionaries.

- Electronic spell checkers.

- Large calculators.

- Access to word processing with on-screen word grids.

- Lower case keyboards.

- Give clear instructions in chunks.

- Allow time for processing information.

- Write the words as dictated by the child.

- Teach children how to use mind maps, spider webs, bullet points, flow charts, ICT software, e.g. Clicker 5, 2Simple, Kidspiration.

- Use Cloze procedures.

- Provide alternatives to written tasks where appropriate, for example, a pictorial story map, a flow chart or a diagram.

- Have appropriate expectations, differentiated objectives with clear success criteria presented visually or verbally focusing on the process rather than the product.

Difficulties with reading, writing, spelling and maths

- Use verbal encouragement and feedback on learning given throughout the duration of the task.

- Use coloured markers for whiteboard work. Try writing alternate lines in a different colour.

- Plan seating purposely to provide opportunities within the daily routine for mixed ability paired reading and recording.

- Organise seating for the child to ensure that they can see you, the whiteboard and the visual prompts.

- When working on tasks that are not specifically linked to literacy or numeracy skills, consider organising children into mixed ability groups.

- Remember to mark for content, rather than spelling or presentation.

- Use a highlighter or a dot to mark spelling errors that have been taught.

▭ Develop a supportive classroom ethos

- Promote an understanding of the barriers some children have to reading, writing and spelling.

- Seek to create an environment where children support and encourage one another.

- Seek to value the contribution of all children.

- Use praise and reward appropriately.

Having read through the information on dyslexia, dyscalculia and dysgraphia and the strategies for providing appropriate support for children with these needs, turn to Chapter 7: The inclusive learning environment (page 67). This provides more specific information on developing an inclusive classroom. A list of suggested resources is provided on pages 77–79. The resources are colour-coded to match the colours for each area of need in this book.

5 Dyspraxia or Developmental Coordination Disorder (DCD)

What is dyspraxia?

'Dyspraxia is an impairment or immaturity of the organisation of movement. Associated with this there may be problems of language, perception and thought.'

(Dyspraxia Foundation)

Dyspraxia or Developmental Coordination Disorder (DCD) is often described as the 'hidden difficulty'. It has been, and still is, overlooked or misinterpreted in young children. It is a condition that can have a significant impact on children's education and well-being. It affects between 2 and 10% of the population and boys are four times more likely to be affected than girls. Some very early signs of dyspraxia can be irritability at birth, poor feeding, poor sleeping and slowness to achieve milestones such as crawling, walking, hopping, jumping, sitting and walking up and down stairs.

Dyspraxia is not due to a general medical condition, such as cerebral palsy. In children with dyspraxia, there appears to be an immaturity in the way the brain processes information which results in messages from the brain to the muscles not being properly or fully transmitted. Performance in daily life skills such as dressing, feeding, walking, running, etc., in fact, any activity that requires coordinated physical movements or that requires gross and fine motor coordination is substantially below age-related expectations. This is a lifelong disability which can improve as the child grows older. Improvement is largely due to regular exercising – often directed by an occupational therapist – but also due to the child developing personal strategies to help them deal with the difficulty. Dyspraxia significantly impedes academic achievement. There can be significant difficulties, not just with handwriting (a skill that requires fine motor coordination) but also in the speed of processing information. Dyspraxia affects the planning of what the child does and how they do it.

With very young children, we can very easily overlook some of the symptoms and there is almost an acceptance of a child's 'clumsiness'. 'Oh, he's a bit clumsy but he'll grow out of it' is an expression often used by teachers and parents.

It is imperative that we do not overlook the early signs!

Dyspraxia or Developmental Coordination Disorder (DCD)

The development of gross and fine motor skills

At various stages of development, children would be expected to demonstrate the following **gross motor skills**:

36–48 months

- Run around furniture and people.
- Walk along a line.
- Balance on one foot for five to ten seconds.
- Jump up and down on the spot on both feet.
- Ride a three-wheeled bike.
- Climb up the steps and slide down a slide independently.
- Jump over a low object and land on both feet together.
- Throw a ball overhead.
- Catch a bouncing ball.
- Crawl through a tunnel.

48–60 months

- Walk forwards, backwards and sideways.
- Walk backwards toe-heel.
- Hop on one foot.
- Jump forward ten times without falling.
- Walk up and down stairs independently, alternating feet.
- Do a somersault.
- Catch a ball thrown by an adult.

Dyspraxia or Developmental Coordination Disorder (DCD)

Children would be expected to demonstrate the following **fine motor skills**:

By 48 months

- Build a tower of nine small blocks.
- Put pegs into a peg board.
- Make a circle on paper, in the sand, etc.
- Manipulate dough/clay materials (rolls balls, snakes, cakes).
- Hold a pencil with appropriate grip.
- Pour water from a jug with a spout into a large container.

By 60 months

- Use scissors to cut on a line continuously.
- Copy a cross.
- Copy a square.
- Draw a person with a head and at least two body parts.
- Thread beads onto a lace.
- Write some letter shapes and numerals.
- Dress themselves (with the minimum support).

If children are not achieving the expected progress in the development of their fine and gross motor skills, this could be an early sign that the child may have dyspraxia. The school's SENCO should be informed so that appropriate action can be taken in line with the SEN Code of Practice. Some older children within your class may have difficulties in the following areas:

- **Perception:** judging position and distance between themselves in relation to other people and objects.
- **Ocular motor control:** visual tracking, left to right.
- **Orientation:** reversal of letters.
- **Figure ground differentiation:** difficulty in identifying the small from the large, e.g. picking out one animal from a tray of assorted animals.

Dyspraxia or Developmental Coordination Disorder (DCD)

- **Vestibular system:** the inner ear detects the movements of the head. It works with the visual system to help us detect speed of movement, helping us to stay upright against gravity and to keep our balance.

- **Proprioception:** messages from our muscles and joints tell us where our limbs and other body parts are. Children with poor proprioception need to get feedback to confirm where their body parts are.

- **Muscle tone:** postural stability. Muscle tone can be under-developed.

- **Laterality:** left/right confusion, direction, strength.

- **Bilateral integration:** using right and left limbs in combination or opposition.

- **Motor planning:** difficulty in carrying out activities or instructions. Not able to generalise or memorise movements, e.g. riding a bike.

From Year 1, the classroom teacher would expect children to be able to do the following:

- Sit still.
- Pay attention.
- Use a pencil or pen.
- Visually track along a page.
- Organise thoughts, emotions and behaviour.
- Make decisions.
- Develop capacity for abstract thought and reasoning.
- Coordinate movements for physical activities such as P.E.

All of these activities/skills are dependent on well-developed coordination. For the child with dyspraxia, the teacher needs to have an understanding of the impact that **not** being able to do these activities/skills has on their learning.

Verbal dyspraxia

Verbal dyspraxia is a difficulty in coordinating the movements required for producing clear speech sounds and in sequencing sounds together in words. The child's speech can often be described as 'unintelligible', even to family members. A speech therapist may describe this as having oro-motor difficulties, which affect the coordination of the lips, tongue, palate and larynx.

Children with verbal dyspraxia may have:

● A family history of speech, language or literacy difficulties.

● Delayed language development – expressive language usually more affected than receptive language.

● Delayed development of early speech skills, e.g. babbling.

● Feeding difficulties.

● Slow movement of the lips and/or tongue.

● Fine and gross motor difficulties.

● Excessive salivation.

Some children can present with verbal dyspraxia but not necessarily exhibit other characteristics of dyspraxia, as mentioned above. Each child will be unique in the way their difficulties present. For example, some children may have difficulties with gross motor skills (they trip, bump into things, etc.) but might be able to organise themselves effectively. Others may have difficulties with fine motor movements (they cannot thread beads, do jigsaws, etc.) but have good spatial awareness and move around the classroom without bumping into objects, people and furniture.

◖ Impact of dyspraxia on the physical and emotional well being of children

A recent study from the Dyspraxia Foundation, which helps more than 10,000 families a year, supports previous research showing that young people are at risk of experiencing social and emotional difficulties and rising obesity levels as a result. Children with dyspraxia are three times more likely to be overweight than their typically developing peers.

From a very young age, children experiencing coordination difficulties become very aware of their differences. Activities requiring good coordinated movement like riding a bicycle, catching a ball, playing board games, etc., become too great a challenge and are often avoided. This can lead them to become isolated from their peers, either by their own choice, or exclusion by others because they cannot keep up with the rest of the group. Daily activities such as getting dressed, walking, running, climbing and eating may take a significantly longer time than for other children. Children with dyspraxia are often slow, late or last. This can have a significant impact on their self-esteem and emotional well being and contribute to feelings of loneliness and social isolation.

Dyspraxia or Developmental Coordination Disorder (DCD)

They often look unhappy. They are at significant risk of becoming socially excluded in later life. As they get older, their frustration can lead to behavioural difficulties. Where dyspraxia is not identified early enough, there is a danger of the teacher focusing their attention on the child's behaviour rather than on the underpinning causes.

Children with dyspraxia are less likely to participate in physical activities such as cycling, football and other sports clubs, because activity leaders generally do not provide the support and understanding that they need in order to achieve and progress. Being appropriately supported to be able to participate in P.E. lessons, team sports and other leisure activities can be a first step in helping children with dyspraxia to become physically active.

Children today are very much immersed in a technological world. Sitting at a computer or a games console have become common pastimes for all children. Although there are opportunities for children to engage in physical play by joining after school activities, the freedom for children to play out on their own with their friends (without supervision) seems to have diminished over the years. Children seem to take less time and opportunity to participate in activities that will help them to develop their physical skills and coordination. For children with dyspraxia it is even more tempting not to join in with physical activities because their difficulties significantly inhibit their performance.

Why is good coordination important?

We need good coordination in order to carry out the activities of everyday living. It underpins all learning activities. If children experience barriers to carrying out everyday tasks then self-esteem and emotional well being becomes affected. For example, a child may be given a writing task to complete within a given time. The child with dyspraxia may struggle with a range of skills that other children do with ease, such as finding their pen and book, moving around the classroom negotiating the space to avoid bumping into furniture, remembering where to begin their writing and what they have to write, trying to remember the orientation of individual letters and coordinating their movements in order to hold their pen correctly. The child with dyspraxia will take longer than others to complete the task and probably won't complete it at all. They may, after all this effort, produce a piece of work that is poorly presented and difficult to read. It is of little wonder that their self-esteem might be greatly affected by this lack of success despite the amount of effort expended on the task.

◻ Long-term effects of dyspraxia

Dyspraxia is a lifelong disability. Children who live with this daily challenge can often grow up with the effects of having low confidence levels and low self-esteem. Without appropriate support they can become disaffected at school which then leads to a range of associated behaviours such as refusing to attend, being easily led by others in order to gain friendship and poor academic performance. This will have a profound effect on how they approach the daily challenges of life when they become adults.

In summary

Good coordination skills are essential for future academic success. Our feelings, experiences and thoughts exist in the skin, joints and muscles as much as in the brain. Early identification of dyspraxia in the early years is essential if we are to make a difference. Teachers themselves can do so much for children with dyspraxia without the need to wait for a therapist to give advice. This can be achieved by implementing the strategies on page 57 and by gaining a sound understanding of the condition and the impact it can have on everyday living and learning.

Ben's story

Hi, my name is Ben and I have dyspraxia. I am nine years old and go to a primary school close to where I live. We moved here about six months ago so I'm quite new to the school. I would like to tell you what it's like to have dyspraxia.

I get up at 7 am every day. My Mum wakes me up and asks me to wash my face and hands, get dressed and come down for breakfast. My Mum lays my clothes out for me and puts them in the order in which I have to put them on and puts them the right way round so I can put them on more easily. If she didn't do this I'd probably forget to put my pants on before I put my trousers on or something like that.

I always make a bit of a mess in the bathroom when I'm washing. I get water everywhere but I don't get into trouble for it. I used to get told off all the time because my Mum just thought I was messing about.

I go down for breakfast and it's usually all ready for me. My mum has started letting me pour my own cereal and milk now. I'm getting better at it because I don't spill as much any more. My Mum then asks me to brush my teeth and comb my hair, then she helps me pack my bag for school. She asks me to go and get my planner which helps me to remember what I need to take.

Dyspraxia or Developmental Coordination Disorder (DCD)

We set off for school a bit earlier than everyone else because I'm a slow walker. My Mum still takes me to the edge of the school playground and waits till I meet my friend Sam.

I love my Mum, she really understands me.

When it's time to go into school, I go in with Sam. I take my coat off and hang it up, it used to take me ages to do this and I was always last. I'm much better now and Sam always helps by putting my lunch box on the shelf for me.

I don't really like school. I'm not good at anything, really. I always seem to be last at everything and the other kids in my class get annoyed if they have to wait for me. My teacher doesn't really understand what it's like to have dyspraxia and I'm sure she thinks I'm just lazy and stubborn, but I'm not. I don't find the work hard but I get loads of it and I never seem to be able to finish it. My handwriting isn't very good and I always have to do it again. Everyone in my class can use a pen to write with but I still have to use a pencil because I can't write joined up. I find this really hard and I wish I didn't have to do as much writing. If we are doing a worksheet, I get really annoyed because I know the answers but I never get to show that I can answer them because I never finish it. I miss my playtime when I don't finish.

I'm beginning to hate school more and more because I just can't seem to do anything right. I really only have Sam as a friend. He talks a bit funny but I understand him. He has a helper. The other boys in the class don't really want to play with me. They all play football but I'm not very good so they leave me out.

My Mum was called into school last week because I was getting a bit cheeky to the teacher. I do this a lot more now because it makes the other boys in the class laugh and they think I'm cool. I know I shouldn't do it but I am getting fed up of everything and don't care about school. I want to go back to my old school.

My Mum has tried to explain to my teacher about dyspraxia but for some reason she doesn't understand. My last teacher did and she really helped me. Mum is going to meet with Mrs Kay next week. She works with lots of kids in school who need a bit of help.

I just want to be like everyone else!

By the time I get home I'm really tired and in a bad mood because I've probably been in trouble. My Mum gives me a hug and lets me sit and watch TV. I'm too tired to do anything else.

I love my Mum!!

Dyspraxia or Developmental Coordination Disorder (DCD)

 Suggested strategies

- Differentiate the activity by length of time/speed, size of resources, space.

- Ensure success and completion of tasks by:

  ○ Providing appropriate support, e.g. adult completes half a jigsaw and then asks the child to finish the jigsaw.

  ○ Being clear about what you want the child to learn. Act as a scribe if necessary, e.g. in a maths activity, a child is asked to count a number of objects, adult records.

- Provide a range of resources for writing to meet the needs of children who find writing physically difficult.

  ○ Practise multi-sensory letter formation, e.g. sandpaper letters, sky writing, rice, sand trays.

  ○ Use pencil grips, writing lines, stencils.

- Ensure a good seating position, e.g. an appropriate size of table and chair. Feet need to be firmly on the ground. When sitting on a carpet, provide a designated space or use a sitting mat or a cushion.

- Provide desktop texts to copy from if necessary.

- Provide written copies of homework tasks, and reminder prompts that will support the child remembering information.

- Assist children's stability by allowing them to rest against something when sitting on the carpet. Allow them to sit with legs out straight. Always provide a seat with a back, not a stool.

- Provide regular opportunities for children to be first – finished, dressed, in the line, etc.

- Provide resources to assist personal organisation ranging from a series of three sequenced photographs/pictures to a 'to do' list or personal planner.

- Provide a range of equipment for physical activities to make movements larger and/or slower, e.g. large soft balls, balloons and scarves.

- Provide opportunities in physical activities to work at floor level, e.g. slide on tummy, crawling, sitting and rolling a ball to partner.

- Provide opportunities and activities to promote body awareness, resistance, pushing and pulling and cross lateral movement, e.g. large sheets of lycra.

Dyspraxia or Developmental Coordination Disorder (DCD)

Key principle

- Ensure that the child has the opportunity to choose their play partner or team members when taking part in planned physical activities.

- Provide activities and resources that will strengthen the child's hands, e.g. squeeze a soft ball, use tongs to pick up small objects, pop bubble wrap.

- Provide opportunities for exercising before using writing/drawing implements.

- Provide continuous prompts, reminders and praise.

> Start big – aim small
> Start low – aim high

What to avoid

- Unnecessary physical barriers in the classroom.

- Limit the number of steps in a task, e.g. do not expect the child to write their name, date and title before beginning the planned task.

- Unnecessary formal paper based handwriting activities.

- Unrealistic expectations, e.g. limit time on the carpet, sitting for long periods, insisting on a certain position (legs crossed).

- Situations where the child is always being last or late.

- Situations where the child with motor difficulty is left waiting to be selected for P.E. activities.

- Disturbing the child when on task.

- Using fluorescent lighting or fluttering ceiling displays.

Having read through the information on dyspraxia and the strategies for providing appropriate support for children with these needs, turn to Chapter 7: The inclusive learning environment (page 67). This provides more specific information on developing an inclusive classroom. A list of suggested resources is provided on pages 77–79. The resources are colour-coded to match the colours for each area of need in this book.

6 Attention Deficit (Hyperactivity) Disorder (AD(H)D)

AD(H)D

Attention Deficit Hyperactivity Disorder (AD(H)D) and Attention Deficit Disorder (ADD) refer to a range of behaviours associated with poor attention span. Some of the signs of (AD(H)D) might be:

- Inattentiveness
- Hyperactivity
- Restlessness
- Impulsiveness

These behaviours often prevent children from learning and socialising. AD(H)D is sometimes called **hyperkinetic disorder**. About 1.7 per cent of the UK population, mostly children, have ADD or AD(H)D. Boys are more likely to be affected.

The symptoms of AD(H)D

Inattentiveness

A child must have displayed at least six of the following symptoms for at least six months and in two different settings, i.e. home and school. These symptoms need to be present to such an extent that it is unusual for their age and level of intelligence.

- Fails to pay close attention to detail or makes careless mistakes when undertaking school work or while playing.
- Inability to complete tasks or sustain attention in play activities.
- Appears not to listen to what is said.
- Fails to follow through instructions.
- Disorganised when going about tasks and activities.
- Avoids tasks, like homework, that require sustained mental effort.
- Loses things necessary for certain tasks or activities, such as pencils, books or toys.
- Easily distracted.
- Forgetful in the course of daily activities.

Hyperactivity and restlessness

A child must have displayed at least three of the following symptoms for at least six months to an extent that it is unusual for their age and level of intelligence:

- Runs around or climbs over things excessively.
- Unduly noisy in playing; finds it hard to play quietly.

- Stands up and wanders around in the classroom or in other situations where staying seated is expected.

- Fidgets with hands or feet or wriggles on seat.

Impulsivity

At least one of the following symptoms must have persisted for at least six months to an extent that is unusual for their age and level of intelligence:

- Blurts out answers and interrupts before the questions have been finished.

- Finds waiting and turn taking extremely difficult.

- Interrupts or intrudes on others, e.g. butts into others' conversations or games.

- Talks excessively and doesn't seem to be able to stop even when asked.

Attention difficulties and hyperactivity

For a diagnosis or description of AD(H)D a child would be expected to show the above difficulties in more than one setting, e.g. at school and at home.

Sometimes problems are not shown at home but are very evident when a child is in another situation, e.g. at the doctor's or in shops. Parents do not always realise that their child's behaviour is different from what would normally be expected of children of a similar age – perhaps because they have no other children, or they have other children who behave similarly. It may also be that the problems are mild or the family has handled the lack of concentration and inattentiveness at home in such a way that it is not evident that there is a major problem, or because the child is very young. In these cases it is quite reasonable for parents not to consider that their child has an attention deficit problem.

What else could it be?

Children can display symptoms of AD(H)D when in fact there may be other explanations for their behaviour, such as:

- Grand mal or petit mal epileptic seizures can cause a child to become drowsy, limiting their attention. Epilepsy can also cause unusual behaviour.

- Hearing problems, such as deafness or glue ear, making it hard for a child to follow instructions and make them appear inattentive.

- Reading problems, making it hard to complete tasks or follow instructions.

- Obsessive compulsive disorder leads to people following strange rituals that preoccupy their thoughts and distract their attention.

- Tourette's syndrome involves repetitive, involuntary jerking movements of the body and sudden outbursts of noise or swearing.

- Autism and Asperger's Syndrome often lead to difficulties in understanding and using language.

- Prolonged periods of insufficient sleep can cause poor concentration.

NB: Many children may be very active, may be easily distracted or have difficulty concentrating. If these behaviours are relatively mild, they should not be considered a disorder.

What other difficulties can occur alongside AD(H)D?

AD(H)D often occurs alongside other difficulties and is not the sole cause of problem behaviour. Children may have temper tantrums, sleep disorders and be clumsy. Other behavioural problems that occur with AD(H)D include:

- **Confrontational** defiant behaviour, which occurs in 60 per cent of children. The child loses their temper, argues and refuses to comply with adults and deliberately annoys others.

- **Conduct disorders** occur in at least 25 per cent of children. The child may be destructive or show deceitful behaviour such as lying, breaking rules and stealing.

- **Specific learning difficulties**, including dyslexia, occur in 25–30 per cent of children.

- **Severe clinical depression** occurs in 33 per cent of children.

- **Anxiety disorders** occur in 30 per cent of children.

(Dr Helen Likierman, 2005)

What causes AD(H)D?

Research suggests that there is no single cause for AD(H)D. Some studies suggest that it is a disorder which affects several areas of the brain that are responsible for controlling the regulation of behaviour, working memory, thinking, planning and organising. Certain physical or biological factors can be causes of AD(H)D, such as the child's temperament, as this contributes to their attitude and personality. A number of factors can impact upon the early development of the brain. Exposure of the foetus to toxic substances such as alcohol, tobacco and lead, brain injuries due to birth trauma, etc., can contribute to the development of AD(H)D. There may be a hereditary link. AD(H)D is more prevalent in boys. Studies do not support the idea that AD(H)D is the result of poor parenting practices or other family environment variables.

Children with AD(H)D present a considerable challenge to teachers and parents, but they bring many positive qualities to the classroom too:

- Curiosity
- Inventiveness and creativity
- Spontaneity
- Boundless energy and enthusiasm
- Humour

Children with AD(H)D can easily fall into a cycle of poor behaviour, followed by criticism, which makes them feel bad about themselves, which then leads to further poor behaviour. Instead, try to provide positive reinforcement of their strengths, to make the child feel better and motivate them to behave well. It's important to focus on the child's strengths and, by praising and rewarding good behaviour, their confidence and self-esteem will be boosted. Supporting children with AD(H)D and helping them to recognise aspects of their day that may prove difficult for them, will help them to begin to manage their own behaviour.

Teachers need to anticipate and plan for intervention!

The following chart will help you track (over a period of time) the behaviours presented by the child. It will help in making decisions on whether or not it is necessary to take further action in determining the needs of the child.

Teachers can support the inclusion of children with AD(H)D by implementing the strategies on page 65.

Attention Deficit (Hyperactivity) Disorder (AD(H)D)

AD(H)D Behavioural Tracking Sheet

● Green dot – Rarely   ● Yellow dot – Sometimes   ● Red dot - Often

	Mon		Tues		Wed		Thur		Fri	
	AM	PM	AM	PM	AM	PM	AM	PM	AM	PM
Hyperactivity /impulsiveness										
Fidgeting										
Moves when attempting to sit still										
Incessant movement										
Talks excessively										
Interrupts when others are talking										
Inability to wait their turn										
Attention skills										
Limited attention										
Flitting from activity to another										
Easily distracted										
Poor personal organisation skills										
Forgets instructions and routines										
Doesn't finish tasks										
Observation notes										

Attention Deficit (Hyperactivity) Disorder (AD(H)D)

Let Simon tell you about his world. Simon is ten years old and has AD(H)D.

Simon's story

I'm standing outside the head teacher's office – AGAIN! I'm always here. School sucks! I never seem to be out of trouble. This is the fifth time this week and the head teacher, Mr Hind, wants to know why I've been sent to see him again.

I said, I dunno, it makes the other kids laugh so I do it even more…sorry, Mr Hind.

Even though I said that I was sorry, he said that he was going to ask my parents to come in for a talk. He told me that I had to stop disrupting the class like this.

Next thing I knew, my Mum and Dad came in to school to see Mr Hind and Mrs Williams. I'm not sure why she was there – she always works with the kids who can't read, but I can read really well.

I don't like school now. It never used to be horrible but I just always seem to get into trouble. I just can't seem to stop myself from annoying people and being silly. I have lots of friends, but I think they like me because I do things that they would really like to do but they're too scared. I make them laugh and they get me to do all kinds of things in school to annoy the teachers.

Things are changing though. It's our SATs year and we are being told that we have to really work hard and concentrate to get good marks in our tests. Everyone just keeps talking about SATs! I'm not good at concentrating at all. I just can't stop myself from fidgeting. I hate sitting still – I get really impatient. I know I have to put my hand up and wait my turn but I just can't seem to be able to, so I blurt out the answers. This annoys Mr Dodds, my teacher, and it's starting to annoy the other kids. I usually get sent to sit at the back of the room, but then I fiddle with things and pull faces and make the other kids laugh. I eventually get sent to Mr Hind.

I'm the same at home. My Mum cries a lot and my Dad shouts at me. I spend a lot of time in my room. This makes me angry and I sometimes make it all messy.

My friends usually think I'm cool. I don't really want to be the naughty one but everyone expects me to act silly, so I do!

Mrs Williams came to see me yesterday and told me that a man was coming in to see me to help me with my behaviour and that I would have to visit the hospital. Why? I didn't feel ill. She said it was about my behaviour. I'm really fed up and I don't ever want to go to school again.

I saw the man, went to the hospital to see some more people and now I have to take medicine. They say it will help me concentrate better. Mrs Williams explained to me that I have ADHD and told me about it. She comes to talk to me every morning before I go to class and we talk about what I will be doing that day and how I'm expected to behave. I like this because I know what's going to happen.

I'm standing outside the head teacher's office AGAIN – but this time it's to get a sticker for being good!

Attention Deficit (Hyperactivity) Disorder (AD(H)D)

 ## Suggested strategies

- Sit the child near the teacher but always as a regular part of the class.
- Ensure the child is seated away from distracting stimuli such as heaters, windows or air conditioners.
- Surround the child with good role models or a 'buddy'.
- Encourage peer tutoring and shared learning.
- Ensure that resources are readily available and there are enough to go round.
- Vary the pace of tasks and activities used in lessons.
- Set a variety of tasks and activities – where possible include 'hands on' activities.
- Immediately reward task completion if possible.
- Reduce extraneous background noises.
- Ensure that the child is given clear, concise verbal instructions.
- Make sure you establish eye contact when speaking to the child.
- Get the child to repeat back instructions.
- Use prompt sheets and step-by-step instructions.
- Teach the child strategies to improve their listening skills.
- Encourage the child to take notes.
- Use visual cues.
- Allow the child to fiddle with an agreed object, e.g. a stress ball.
- Anticipate potential problems and have planned responses.
- Emphasise the difference between 'in class' and 'out of class' behaviour.
- Allow the child a calming-down period before coming into the classroom.
- Encourage a calm atmosphere in the classroom.
- Give short breaks between tasks.
- Plan ahead for transition times.
- Use alternative technology, e.g. computer, dictaphone.
- Give the whole class stretching exercises midway through lessons.
- Seek advice from an occupational therapist.
- Encourage the child to do specific jobs which require activity, e.g. hand out books to other children.

- Liaise with parents/carers regarding consistent strategies to help develop a routine.

- Encourage the child to work in a pair with another child.

- Establish and agree with the child a behaviour management programme.

- Provide immediate and consistent feedback regarding behaviour.

- Develop a private signal system with the child to notify them gently when they are off task or acting inappropriately.

- Provide an area for 'time out' within the classroom. Encourage the child to recognise the warning signs and to realise that sometimes it's necessary to stop what they are doing and calm down.

- Give the child time targets – use a timer – to help them keep on task.

- Use rewards appropriate to the child, e.g. star charts, stickers, merits, points systems, goal cards, 'golden time' or choice of activity time.

- Be firm and consistent about established rules, but always stay calm and positive.

- Keep a regular routine in the classroom. Organise resources in a clear, systematic way so that the child can find what they need.

- Avoid ridicule and criticism – keep a sense of humour!

What to avoid

- Challenging the child instead of the behaviour.

- Setting unachievable goals – particularly in workload and in the time needed to complete a task or activity.

- Putting the child in difficult social situations, e.g. they may find whole school assemblies demanding.

- Giving too many sanctions and consequences for unacceptable actions.

- Setting too many targets for behaviour.

- Expecting prolonged periods of sitting, waiting, etc.

- Unrealistic expectations – acknowledge the child's symptoms.

Having read through the information on Attention Deficit (Hyperactivity) Disorder and the strategies for providing appropriate support for children with AD(H)D, turn to Chapter 7: The inclusive learning environment (page 67). This provides more specific information on developing an inclusive classroom. A list of suggested resources is provided on pages 77–79. The resources are colour-coded to match the colours for each area of need in this book.

7 The inclusive learning environment

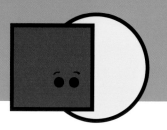

All children must have their basic needs met if they are to grow and learn.

We need to create an inclusive learning environment in which all children:

● Have their basic physiological needs met (space, light, water and food).

● Feel safe and secure, e.g. having their own designated space where they can keep their own belongings safe.

● Know they are part of a supportive group where children help one another and adults are warm and responsive.

● Know that their individual strengths and differences are valued.

● Have access to a range of learning opportunities and resources that support them to achieve their full potential.

The language we use on a day-to-day basis can impact on the learning environment we create within our own classrooms.

'I have come to the frightening conclusion that I am the decisive element in the classroom. It is my personal approach that creates the climate. As a teacher I possess tremendous power to make a child's life miserable or joyous. I can be a tool of torture or an instrument of inspiration. I can humiliate, humour, hurt or heal.'
(Ginott 1972. Teacher and child. New York: Macmillan.)

The inclusive learning environment

The role of the adult in creating an inclusive learning environment

- To promote a shared understanding of difference and diversity.

- To provide open-ended resources that will support the development of creativity and problem-solving skills.

- To provide differentiated material, resources and equipment that will enable children to progress to the next steps in their learning.

- To support children to achieve their aims by intervening sensitively when appropriate.

- To scaffold children's learning so that they can achieve, with help, what they may be able to do on their own tomorrow.

- To share ideas, thoughts and experiences with children.

- To be a positive role model.

- To give feedback on their achievements.

- To support children to develop the meta-cognitive skills necessary to analyse and discuss their own learning.

- To observe children's development and to use this information to plan effectively for future developments.

'...day to day engagement of children and adults in shared activities contributes to the rapid progress of children in becoming skilled participants in the intellectual and social lives of their society...like genes, social interaction and social arrangements are an essential aspect of child development, without which it would be impossible to conceive of a child developing.'

(Rogoff 1990. Apprenticeship in thinking. Oxford: Oxford University Press)

Creating an accessible inclusive learning environment

First, kneel down or sit at a table and look around the classroom from a child's point of view and see what the space looks, feels and sounds like. Ask yourself the following questions:

- Is the classroom light, tidy and inviting to walk into?

- Is space and furniture arranged appropriately to meet the needs of children with physical or mobility challenges?

- Are there identifiable areas within the classroom?

- Are the areas of the classroom clearly labelled with pictures and/or symbols and words?

The inclusive learning environment

- Is there a designated space for children to store personal items?

- Can all the children reach resources and materials?

- Are there clearly defined areas to display and celebrate children's work?

- Are displays over-stimulating, cluttered or worn?

- Are displays multi-sensory?

- Is there a visual timetable displayed at child height?

- Is there an area where children can go to relax and be quiet?

- Is the classroom furniture of an appropriate height and size?

- Are materials, cushions and rugs used to deaden classroom noise?

- Are children surrounded by primary colours that can be over-stimulating?

- Are children surrounded by the calming colours of nature (greens, blues, browns, creams) ?

- Are there systems in place for children to find and replace resources independently?

- Are objects of reference or visual representations used to support children's understanding of the association between objects, photographs, pictures, symbols and the resources and equipment available to them?

- Are visual behaviour prompts used to support children with challenging behaviour?

- Is there a range of resources available for writing and mark making such as paper in a selection of colours and sizes, whiteboards, chalks, big brushes, pens and paper?

- Are there alternative means for children to record their work, e.g. a dictaphone or computer?

- Is there a limited number of front-facing books on display in the book area?

- Are there published and made books available that relate to the specific theme in each of the areas of the classroom?

- Are there learning prompts displayed, e.g. grapheme charts, number lines?

- Are there personal learning prompts, word books and dictionaries available for individual children?

- Is there a listening area where children can listen to pre-recorded stories?

Teachers can use the picture signs (page 70 and on the CD-ROM) to make individual or class visual timetables. The introduction of visual timetables will support all children's understanding of routines and structure within a school day. Displaying the pictorial signs in the classroom areas will help children to understand the association between the visual picture and the equipment available in that specific area of the classroom.

The inclusive learning environment

Picture signs (available on the CD-ROM)

Picture signs which correspond to areas of the classroom and to curriculum areas are available on the CD. These are available in a variety of sizes:

1 label on A4 sheet (A4 size 297mm x 210mm)   8 labels on A4 sheet (approx. 105mm x 74mm each)
38 labels on A4 sheet (approx. 34mm x 34mm each)   4 labels on A4 sheet (approx. 148mm x 105mm each)

Some ideas for the classroom

A child in Year 1 independently using an individual visual timetable.

The adult is using a group visual timetable inclusively to support nursery children to plan their day. Within the group there is a child with speech language and communication needs.

The visual timetable has been made using the black and white signs from Communicate: InPrint2 – this is a desktop publishing package that is available from **www.widgit.com**

A class visual timetable helps all children to understand the structure of the daily routine. As the ball is moved along the string throughout the day, children are provided with visual support to help them know what is happening next. The visual timetable has been made using the black and white signs from Communicate: InPrint2 – this is a desktop publishing package that is available from **www.widgit.com**

Storage and retrieval systems using pictures and words

Ensure that all equipment and resources that children can access independently have an identified and clearly labelled storage space. When labelling resources use either a reference object or photograph. Write the name of the resource or equipment clearly next to the photograph. The labels then can be attached to the front of the containers so they are clearly visible to the children. Using different coloured labels to correspond to the areas of the classroom will help children know where different types of resources and equipment are stored. Some children may need additional visual prompts to be able to access resources independently. Consider using simple black and white symbols.

Behaviour prompts (available on the CD-ROM)

The inclusive learning environment

Inclusion checklist (also available on CD-ROM)

Demonstrating inclusion	How do I support this?	How can I develop this?
Example: Children's seating planned carefully. Not all SEN children sitting together.	Yes, I sit a more settled child with a child who finds concentration difficult	Use a 'peer tutoring approach' for ALL learning
Children are clear about the day, e.g. visual timetable displayed.		
Visual prompts are used to aid understanding of instructions.		
Questions are pitched so as to challenge children at all levels.		
Room is clearly labelled with pictorial labels.		
All children are helped to access written text (buddying, adult support, recording).		
Everyone is welcomed into the room.		
Multi-sensory teaching approaches are used.		
Interactive strategies are used to encourage all children to participate, e.g. whiteboards for children to use.		

The Inclusive Learning Environment

Demonstrating inclusion	How do I support this?	How can I develop this?
Pre-teaching offered for those who need it to help with access to lesson.		
Additional adults are actively involved throughout to support all children to access the learning.		
Engagement of all children is done sensitively and supportively, e.g. children given thinking time, partner talk, etc.		
Can ALL children succeed at the task?		
Can ALL children successfully access all areas and activities in the room and can they be successful?		
Do I positively discriminate, e.g. if a child is always last to get dressed, do I allow them more time?		

Epilogue: And what about Harry?

Harry's story

Harry is a child who is 'different'. He seems to display the behaviours of several different areas of need – has a little bit of this and a little bit of that. A bit of 'allsorts', so to speak. Harry is just not like other children. He's just 'Harry'. He has a range of difficulties, not just one. He could be described as having what the experts call 'co-morbidity'. This, in medical terms can be defined as:

> The presence of one or more disorders (or diseases) in addition to a primary disease or disorder or the interactive effect of such additional disorders or diseases.

There are lots of children like Harry, who presents as a child with 'a little bit of this and a little bit of that'. We meet them regularly in our classrooms. They're not just one shape but lots of different shapes and may be different shapes on different days.

Harry presents his teachers with a range of challenges. Some might say 'problems' but we must not think of these children as 'problems' but as challenges.

Harry has lots of barriers to overcome in his everyday life. Activities and tasks that most children take for granted are impeded by a range of obstacles.

Harry has been diagnosed as having ASD, AD(H)D and dyspraxia. If we consider the impact a single disorder has on a child, what must it be like for Harry?

We have to find out what life is like for Harry and understand his needs before we can provide successful interventions.

Harry is a child who likes routines and finds change difficult to manage. He can be quite impulsive in his behaviour and doesn't think before he acts. In addition to this he has poor coordination and organisational skills.

It is important to find out how Harry learns. What barriers will there be for Harry in terms of accessing the curriculum? What can we do about it? Our expectations will have to change significantly for Harry if we are to include him successfully.

All children are unique. Children with Special Educational Needs are our 'square pegs'. The learning environment we offer to Harry and all other children should be differentiated appropriately and our expectations should be realistic.

Epilogue: And what about Harry?

How do we meet Harry's needs?

We have to start somewhere. The first question to ask is:

What is the main barrier to Harry's learning?

In Harry's case it is his autism. He won't sit with the other children and wanders off to other parts of the classroom. This disrupts the class routine and disturbs the other children and prevents Harry from accessing the lesson. Deal with this first, for example:

● Provide him with a 'fiddle' toy.

● Give him a designated place to sit on the carpet (with his own mat).

● Have a sand timer available so he can see how long he has to sit.

● Provide a related activity for him to access in a different area of the classroom (his favourite place or his own work station).

This would be the main focus for intervention but other strategies could run alongside to address his other areas of need, and try your best to implement the others. In time it will be possible to shift the focus onto other areas of need.

We should anticipate and plan for our 'square pegs' and make reasonable adjustments to the 'round holes'. This is successful inclusion.

Resources

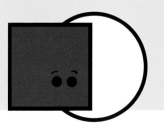

A5 Talking Photo Album
Record your stories, timetables or messages with the Talking Photo Album. Simply insert drawings or photographs into the plastic wallets and record up to a ten second message on every page to support the image/text. **www.tts-group.co.uk**

Hear Myself Sound Phone
Children can hear themselves speak, therefore focusing on every sound they make with this ingenious 'phone'. **www.tts-group.co.uk**

Kidspiration3
For ages four to nine; Kidspiration develops literacy, numeracy and thinking skills using proven visual learning principles. **www.taglearning.com**

2Create A Superstory
A complete tool for personalised multimedia story creation. It helps to inspire children's writing through the use of versatile tools and templates. **www.2simplehome.com**

2Type
Seven programs for learners of all ages to develop keyboard skills and spelling patterns. **www.2simplehome.com**

Crick's Clicker 5
This writing support tool provides on-screen word banks with integrated speech within an easy-to-use talking word processor. The unique Clicker Grids enable children to produce a piece of writing. **www.cricksoft.com/uk**

Lexion
Lexion makes it easy to assess pupils who are struggling with reading and writing. Simply select a test for their age and area of difficulty and Lexion will analyse the result, displaying the results in charts and text. It then automatically creates exercises to address the difficulty. The pupil can practise the exercises either at school or at home and as they improve, they can be re-tested to assess progress. **www.inclusive.co.uk**

RM Maths
RM Maths gives pupils 15 minutes of individualised maths support a day, exactly matched to their ability, with focus on core skills and mental maths. **www.rm.com**

Reading Windows
Support for children who have problems with visual tracking and need a line finder to help guide them down a page of text. **www.tts-group.co.uk**

Reading Rulers
Many children, especially those with dyslexia, have difficulty reading black text on a white background. These coloured rulers have been an enormous help to many with close-reading difficulties. Children say that the change in colour 'stops the words moving about', and 'makes the letters clearer'. Cheaper and more discreet than tinted lenses, these rulers come in five colours so each child can find which works best. **www.tts-group.co.uk**

Autism Starter Kit
This starter kit contains a range of communication tools and stories to help children with autism learn how to deal with social situations. **www.tts-group.co.uk**

Boardmaker v.6 for Windows - UK Edition
Boardmaker gives educators the ability to create a wide range of materials with its wide range of time-saving tools and features. **www.mayer-johnson.co.uk**

Communicate: InPrint2
Symbol-supported desktop publishing
Communicate: In Print 2 is a desktop publishing program for creating symbol-supported resources for printing. It is supplied with the full Widgit Symbol set. Makes visual timetables, flashcards and worksheets quickly and easily. **www.widgit.com**

Desktop Visual Timetable Holder
The perspex holder with velcro strips that can be used to display a child's individual routine or to display step by step instructions in a photographic or written form. **www.spacekraft.co.uk**

Timed Activity Schedule
The combined visual timetable and digital timer helps the child to complete tasks independently. **www.pecs.org.uk**

Privacy Partition
This handy cardboard partition can be placed on a desk to provide an instant visual distraction free work zone. **www.spacekraft.co.uk**

Time Tracker
Will help keep children on track. It has easily programmable green, yellow and red sections and six sounds to indicate the time allocated. **www.spacekraft.co.uk**

Fiddly Fidget
Made from stretchy, washable material, the Fiddly Fidget is brightly coloured and an ideal item for fidgets to fiddle with. Approximately 160mm in diameter. **www.spacekraft.co.uk**

Fuzzy Tangle
A multisensory fiddle toy. **www.sensetoys.com**

Glitter Tubes Pack
A resource which can be used to help concentration as the child focuses on the movements of the glitter and colour particles. They can also be used to calm children or as a turn-taking aid. **www.ldalearning.com**

Squease Jacket
Combines a soft and comfortable hooded sweatshirt with an inflatable Deep Pressure vest. The application of Deep Pressure can help people with sensory processing issues. **www.squeasewear.nl**

Proloquo2Go is an iPhone and iPad application
The app. features natural sounding text-to-speech voices, language symbols and a default vocabulary of over 7,000 words. The current version has adult male/female and boy/girl voices and comes with British English. The app. allows the user to tap a series of symbols that are then placed into the message box, and the sentence is spoken by the chosen voice. Users can even create and store regular sentences to their library for fast and easy access to commonly used phrases. **www.therapy-box.co.uk, Prologue2go.aspx**

Air Cushion
Can be used for balance training in standing, kneeling or seated, BUT can also be used to give improved sensory and proprioception feedback when used as a set cushion for children struggling with concentration or fidgeting. **www.specialdirect.com**

Tri-Go Grip
A unique design that lets the fingertips actually touch the writing implement. Reduces muscle strain and fatigue, whilst ensuring an efficient, comfortable hold. **www.ldalearning.com**

KatchaKup
This classic children's game is good for developing hand-eye co-ordination. Simply swing the tethered ball up in the air and catch it. **www.ldalearning.com**

Tai Chi Wobbler
Three games in one that will develop balance, touch sensitivity and gross motor skills. Children stand on the board and roll the ball along the patterned orbit by swaying the body. **www.ldalearning.com**

■ **Parachutes**
www.tts-group.co.uk

■ **Closing the Gap with Numicon**
A resource kit to help develop a sound foundation of basic number. Designed for children of any age who are experiencing significant difficulties in maths. **www.numicon.com**

Helpful books and websites

■ **ADHD: A Path to Success**
Most AD(H)D books rehash the same worn out theories and treatments. Instead, AD(H)D: A path to success offers a new and refreshing perspective on AD(H)D that makes sense with your own personal daily experience. **www.caer.com**

■ **ADD and ADHD**
A website providing expert advice on making sense of ADD and ADHD. **www.addandadhd.co.uk**

■ **British Dyslexia Association: www.bdadyslexia.org.uk**

■ **Dyspraxia Foundation: www.dyspraxiafoundation.org.uk**

■ **Dyslexia Online Magazine**
Online magazine offering information on and resources for dyslexia.
www.dyslexia-parent.com/magazine.html

■ **Dyslexia Action**
This website provides a wide range of services for children who struggle with literacy. It also provides specialist and short courses in the field of dyslexia for teachers.
www.dyslexiaaction.org.uk

■ **I CAN**
Provides information and resources for parents and practitioners about speech, language and communication difficulties. **www.ican.org.uk**

■ **My Social Stories, edited by Carol Gray and Abbie Leigh White**
The book contains approximately 100 stories and is illustrated throughout with line drawings. It gives ideas for producing personalising social stories. **www.sensetoys.com**

■ **SEN Teacher**
Free teaching resource for Special Educational Needs.

■ **Toe by Toe, by Keda Cowling and Harry Cowling**
A highly structured multi-sensory reading manual for teachers and parents. **www.toebytoe.co.uk**

■ **The National Autistic Society: www.autism.org.uk**

■ **Talking Point**
The first stop for information on children's speech, language and communication development. **www.talkingpoint.org.uk**

■ **The National Autistic Society: Wendy's Webpage**
A fantastic website by Wendy Lawson, a lady with autism. What better way to understand autism than to read about first-hand experiences of living in the world with autism!
www.mugsy.org/wendy

Bibliography

Department for Education (2010). DfE: Special educational needs in England. Retrieved 27 April, 2011, from Department for Education: www.education.gov.uk/rsgateway/DB/SFR/s000939/release.shtml

Department for Education and Skills (2001). The National Numeracy Strategy: Guidance to support pupils with dyslexia and dyscalculia. Nottingham: DfES.

Department for Education (2011). Support and aspiration: A new approach to special educational needs and disability. Retrieved 13 April, 2011, from Department for Education: www.education.gov.uk/childrenandyoungpeople/sen/a0075339/sengreenpaper

Department for Education (2008). Including all learners. Retrieved 16 April, 2011, from Qualifications and Curriculum Development Agency: http://curriculum.qcda.gov.uk

Department for Education and Skills (2001). Special Educational Needs Code of Practice. Nottinghamshire: HMSO.

Dr Helen Likierman, V. M. (2005). ADHD (attention deficit hyperactivity disorder). Retrieved 22 April 2011, from Netdoctor: www.netdoctor.co.uk/diseases/facts/adhd.htm

Dyspraxia Foundation. What is dyspraxia (n.d.). Retrieved 3 March 2001, from Dyspraxia Foundation: http://www.dyspraxiafoundation.org.uk

Ginott, H. (1972). Teacher and child. New York: Free Press.

Goddard-Blythe, S. (2002). Reflexes, learning and behaviour: A window into the child's mind. Fern Ridge Press.

H, A. (1944). Die 'aunstisehen Psychopathen' im Kindesalter. Archiv fur psychiatrie and Nervenkrankheiten 117, 76-136.

I, C. (n.d.). I can evidence. Retrieved 7 December 2010, from I Can: www.ican.org.uk

Kranner, L. (1943). Autistic disturbances of affective contact. Nervous Child 2, 217-250.

Lawson, W. (2006). AS Poetry. London: Jessica Kingsley.

National Autistic Society (2010). Statistics: How many people have autistic spectrum disorder. Retrieved 10 February 2011, from The National Autistic Society website: www.autism.org.uk

National Strategies (2008). Inclusion Development Programme Primary/Secondary: Dyslexia and Speech, Language and Communication Needs. Nottingham: DCSF.

National Strategies (2008). Inclusion Development Programme: Supporting children with speech language and communication needs: Guidance for practitioners in the Early Years Foundation Stage. Nottingham: DCSF.

Primary National Strategies (2005). Learning and teaching for dyslexic children. London: HMSO.

Rogoff, B. (1990). Apprenticeship in thinking. Oxford: Oxford University Press.

Rose, J. (2009). Identifying and teaching children and young people with dyslexia and literacy difficulties. An independent report from Sir Jim Rose to the Secretary of State for Children, Schools and Families. Nottinghamshire: HMSO

Wing, L., & Gould, J. (1979). Severe impairments of social interaction and associated abnormalities in children: epidemiology and classification. Journal of Autism and Developmental Disorders 9, 11-29.